SOCIAL WORK SERIES

BROKEN HOMES

A STUDY OF FAMILY DESERTION AND
ITS SOCIAL TREATMENT

By
JOANNA C. COLCORD

SUPERINTENDENT OF THE CHARITY ORGANIZATION SOCIETY
OF THE CITY OF NEW YORK

NEW YORK
RUSSELL SAGE FOUNDATION
1919

COPYRIGHT, 1919, BY
THE RUSSELL SAGE FOUNDATION

PRINTED MAY, 1919, 2000 COPIES
REPRINTED MARCH, 1921, 1000 COPIES
REPRINTED AUGUST, 1927, 1000 COPIES
REPRINTED NOVEMBER, 1934, 1000 COPIES

WM. F. FELL CO., PRINTERS
PHILADELPHIA

PREFACE

NO LESS thoughtful a critic of men and manners than Joseph Conrad has remarked recently that a universal experience "is exactly the sort of thing which is most difficult to appraise justly in the individual instance." The saying might have been made the motto of this book, for in its pages Miss Colcord—with all the eagerness of the newer school of social workers, bent upon understanding, upon making allowances—seeks that just appraisal to which Conrad refers. Marital infelicities and broken homes are not universal, fortunately, but some of the human weaknesses which lead to them are very nearly so.

To one who brings a long perspective to any theme in social work, Broken Homes suggests the successive stages through which the art of social case work has progressed. Twenty years ago the editor of this Series was responsible for the following sentences in an annual report: "One of our most difficult problems has been how to deal with deserted wives with children. . . . One good woman, whose husband had left her for the second time more than a year ago, declared often and emphatically that she would never let him come back. We rescued her furniture from the landlord, found her work, furnished needed relief, and befriended the chil-

PREFACE

dren; but the drunken and lazy husband returned the other day, and is sitting in the chairs we rescued, while he warms his hands at the fire that we have kept burning."

The passage belongs to the first and what might be termed the "muddling along" period of dealing with family desertion, but the fact that boards of directors actually were willing to print such frank statements about their own shortcomings was a sign that the period was drawing to a close.

This first stage was succeeded by a disciplinary period, in which earnest attempts were made to enact laws that would punish the deserter and aid in his extradition whenever he took refuge across a state line. Laws of the strictest, and these well enforced, seemed for a while the only possible solution.

Then gradually, with the unfolding of a philosophy and a technique of helping people in and through their social relationships, a new way of dealing with this ancient and perplexing human failing was developed. This third way involved a more careful analysis of relationships and motives, a greater variety in approach, an increased flexibility in treatment, a new faith, perhaps, in the re-creative powers latent in human nature. But it is unnecessary to enlarge upon a point of view which these pages admirably illustrate. Desertion laws continue to serve a definite purpose, as Miss Colcord makes clear, but no longer are they either the first or the second resort of the skilful probation officer, family case worker, or child protective agent.

PREFACE

Just after the Russell Sage Foundation published a treatise on Social Diagnosis two years ago, a number of letters came to the author urging that a volume on the treatment of social maladjustments in individual cases follow. But this second subject is not yet ready for the large general treatise. A topic so new as social case treatment must be developed aspect by aspect, preferably in small, practical volumes each written by a specialist. This is such a volume, and Miss Colcord breaks new ground, moreover, in that her book illustrates the whole present trend of social work as applied to individuals.

Grateful acknowledgment should be made to the social case workers who have furnished valuable contributions to the body of data gathered for the present study. Miss Colcord wishes mention made of her especial indebtedness to Miss Betsey Libbey, Miss Helen Wallerstein and Miss Elizabeth Wood of Philadelphia; Mr. C. C. Carstens and Miss Elizabeth Holbrook of Boston; Mrs. A. B. Fox and Mr. J. C. Murphy of Buffalo; Miss Caroline Bedford of Minneapolis; Mr. Stockton Raymond of Columbus; Mrs. Helen Glenn Tyson of Pittsburgh; Mr. Arthur Towne of Brooklyn; Mr. E. J. Cooley, Mr. Charles Zunser, Mr. Hiram Myers, and Miss Mary B. Sayles of New York. Many others not here mentioned were untiring in answering questions and furnishing needed information.

MARY E. RICHMOND
Editor of the Social Work Series

NEW YORK, May, 1919.

CONTENTS

	PAGE
I. INTRODUCTION	7
II. WHY DO MEN DESERT THEIR FAMILIES?	17
III. CHANGES OF EMPHASIS IN TREATMENT	50
IV. FINDING THE DESERTING HUSBAND	65
V. FURTHER ITEMS IN THE INVESTIGATION	91
VI. THE DETAILS OF TREATMENT	106
VII. THE DETAILS OF TREATMENT (*Continued*)	125
VIII. THE HOME-STAYING NON-SUPPORTER	149
IX. NEXT STEPS IN CORRECTIVE TREATMENT	164
X. NEXT STEPS IN PREVENTIVE TREATMENT	185
INDEX	201

BROKEN HOMES

I

INTRODUCTION

IT HAS frequently been said that desertion is the poor man's divorce but, like many epigrams, this one hardly stands the test of experience. When examined closely it is neither illuminating nor, if the testimony of social case workers can be accepted, is it true. It is true, of course, that many of the causes of domestic infelicity which lead to divorce among the well-to-do may bring about desertion among the less fortunate, but the deserting man does not, as a rule, consider his absences from home as anything so final and definite as divorce.

In a study of desertion made by the Philadelphia Society for Organizing Charity in 1902,[*] it

[*] Twenty-fourth Annual Report of the Philadelphia Society for Organizing Charity, p. 25.

BROKEN HOMES

was found that 87 per cent of the men studied had deserted more than once. The combined experience of social workers goes to show that a comparatively small number of first deserters make so complete a break in their marital relations that they are never heard from again, and that an even smaller number actually start new families elsewhere, although no statistical proof of this last statement is available. One social worker of experience says that in her judgment desertion, instead of being a poor man's divorce, comes nearer to being a poor man's vacation.

A man who had always been a good husband and father was discharged from hospital after a long and exhausting illness and returned to his family—wife and seven children—in their five-room tenement. Ten days later he disappeared suddenly, but reappeared some two weeks later in very much better health and ready to resume his occupation and the care of his family. His explanation of his apparent desertion was that he was unable to stand the confusion of his home and "had needed rest." He had "beaten his way" to Philadelphia and visited a friend there.

The reporter of the foregoing remarks that it illustrates "unconscious self-therapy," and that

INTRODUCTION

the patient's disappearance might have been avoided if the services of a good medical-social department had been available at the hospital where the man was treated.

It is more difficult to justify the thirst for experience of another deserting husband who came to the office of a family social agency after an absence of a few months, with effusive thanks for the care of his family and the explanation that he "had always wanted to see the West, and this had been the only way he could find of accomplishing it."

In fact, case work has convinced social workers that there are few things less permanent than desertion. In itself this provisional quality tends to create irritation in the minds of many of the profession. It is upsetting to plan for a deserted family which stops being deserted, so to speak, overnight. But in their understandable despair social workers sometimes overlook essential facts about the nature of marriage. The *permanence* of family life is one of the foundation stones of their professional faith; yet they may fail to recognize certain manifestations

BROKEN HOMES

of this permanence as part and parcel of the end for which they are striving. They would see no point in the practice adopted by a certain social agency which deals with many cases of family desertion. This society, when it has had occasion to print copies of a deserter's photograph to use in seeking to discover his present whereabouts, often presents his wife with an enlargement of the picture suitable for framing. The procedure displays, nevertheless, a profound insight not only into human nature but into the human institution called marriage.

In the next chapter will be considered some of the causes that make men leave their homes. To deal effectively with the situation created by desertion, however, we have need of a wider knowledge than this. Not only what takes men away but what keeps them from going, what brings them back, what leads to their being forgiven and received into their homes again, are matters that seriously concern the social case worker. What is it that makes this plant called marriage so tough of fiber and so difficult to eradicate from even the most unfriendly soil?

INTRODUCTION

It is fortunate (since the majority of case workers are unmarried) that simply to have been a member of a family gives one some understanding of these questions. The theorist who maintains that marriage is purely economic, or that it is entirely a question of sex, has either never belonged to a real family or has forgotten some of the lessons he learned there.

Many volumes have been written upon the history of marriage, or rather of the family, since, as one historian justly puts it, "marriage has its source in the family rather than the family in marriage."* In all these studies the influence of law, of custom, of self-interest, and of economic pressure, is shown to have molded the institution of marriage into curious shapes and forms, some grievous to be borne. But is it not after all the crystallized and conventionalized records of past time which have had to be used as the source material of such studies, and could the spiritual values of the family in

* Goodsell, Willystine: The Family as a Social and Educational Institution, p. 8. New York, The Macmillan Co., 1915.

BROKEN HOMES

any period be found in its laws and learned discourses? We might rather expect to find students of these sources preoccupied with the outward aspects, the failures, the unusual instances. It is as true of human beings as of nations, that the happy find no chronicler. "Out of . . . interest and joy in caring for children in their weakness and watching that weakness grow to strength, family life came into being and has persisted."* It is hardly conceivable that in any society, however primitive, there were not some real families—even when custom ran otherwise—in which marriage meant love and kindness and the mutual sharing of responsibilities. And these families, today as always, are the creators and preservers of the spiritual gains of the human race. It has been beautifully said of the family in such a form, that "it is greater than love itself, for it includes, ennobles, makes permanent, all that is best in love. The pain of life is hallowed by it, the drudgery sweetened, its pleas-

* Byington, Margaret F.: Article on "The Normal Family," *Annals of the American Academy of Political and Social Science*, May, 1918.

INTRODUCTION

ures consecrated. It is the great trysting-place of the generations, where past and future flash into the reality of the present. It is the great storehouse in which the hardly-earned treasures of the past, the inheritance of spirit and character from our ancestors, are guarded and preserved for our descendants. And it is the great discipline through which each generation learns anew the lesson of citizenship that no man can live for himself alone."* It follows that the most trying and discouraging feature of social work with deserted wives; namely, their determination to take worthless men back and back again for another trial, is often only a further manifestation of the extraordinary viability of the family.

It is true that, into this enduring quality, many elements enter, some homely or merely material. A desire for support, or for a resumption of sex relations, may play a part in a wife's decision to forgive the wanderer. There are many other factors—use and wont; pride in being

* Bosanquet, Helen: The Family, p. 342. London, Macmillan & Co., 1906.

BROKEN HOMES

able to show a good front to the neighbors; a feeling that it is unnatural to be receiving support from other sources. Just the mere desire to have his clothes hanging on the wall and the smell of his pipe about, the hundreds of small details that go to make up the habit of living together, have each their separate pull on the woman whose instinct to be wife and mother to her erring man is urging her to give in. Home is, in both their minds,

> ". . . . . the place where when you have to go there
> They have to take you in. . . . .
> Something you somehow haven't to deserve." *

A woman who had left her home town and found clerical work in a strange city, in order not to be near her syphilitic husband from whom she had determined to separate, said, "When you've been married to a man, you can't get over feeling your place is with him."

However we may deplore the results in a given case, the spineless woman who takes her

* Frost, Robert: North of Boston, p. 20. New York, Henry Holt & Co., 1915.

INTRODUCTION

husband back many times may nevertheless be giving a demonstration of the thing we are most interested in conserving—the durability and persistence of the family. And so the social worker who is enabled by experience or imagination to enter into the real meaning of family life is neither scornful nor amused when Mrs. Finnegan is found, on the morning when her case against Finnegan is to come up in the domestic relations court, busily washing and ironing his other shirt in order that he may make a proper appearance and not disgrace the family before the judge.

An attempt will be made in this small book to analyze some causal factors in the problem of the deserter, to touch upon recent changes in the attitude of social workers toward deserted families, to present illustrations from the best discoverable practice in the treatment of desertion, and to suggest certain possible next steps, both on the legal and on the social side. For lack of space, it will be impossible to consider the closely related problems of the deserting wife, the unmarried

BROKEN HOMES

mother, or the divorced couple. It is assumed throughout that the reader is familiar with the general theory of modern case work; and no more is here attempted than to give a number of suggestions which will be found to be practical, it is hoped, when the social worker deals with the home marred and broken by desertion, or when he seeks to prevent this evil by such constructive measures as are now possible.

II

WHY DO MEN DESERT THEIR FAMILIES?

"BEFORE the deserter there was a broken man," said a district secretary who has had conspicuous success in dealing with such men. By this characterization she meant not necessarily a physical or mental wreck, but a man bankrupt for the time being in health, hopes, prospects, or in all three; a man who lacked the power or the will to dominate adverse conditions, who had allowed life to overcome him. Such an unfortunate may not be conscious of his own share in bringing about the difficulties in which he finds himself, but he is always aware that something has gone seriously wrong in his life. His grasp of this fact is the one sure ground upon which the social worker can meet him at the start.

We should distinguish between the *causes* that bring about a given desertion, and the *conscious motives in the mind of the deserter*. It

BROKEN HOMES

is well for the social worker to make the latter the starting point in dealing with the man, accepting the most preposterous as at least worthy of discussion. The absconder is often too inarticulate and ill at ease to give a clear picture of what was in his mind when he went away. If he was out of work, it may have been a perfectly sincere belief that he would find work elsewhere, or perhaps only a speculative hope that he might. (These are not in the beginning genuine desertions, but often become so later on.) It is possible that, beset by irritations and perplexities, the thought of cutting his way out at one stroke from all his difficulties made an appeal too strong to be resisted. Or perhaps he flung out of the house and away, in a passion of anger and jealousy which later crystallized into cold dislike. The spell of an infatuation for another woman might well have been the cause; or he may have been mentally deranged through alcohol. Simple weariness of the burden which he has not strength of body or mind to carry and ought never to have assumed is one attitude to be reckoned with, and failure to realize or in his heart accept the binding nature of his obligations is another.

His temperamental instability may have been such that the desire for a change—the "wanderlust"—was driving him to distraction. Or perhaps, under the urge of his own subconscious feeling of failure, he may have convinced himself that if he could "shake" the old environment and all in it that hampered him, he could take a fresh start and make good. "If I could only get to California," sighed Patrick Donald,* "I have a feeling things would be different." With too much imagination to be content with the situation in which he found himself, Donald had not imagination enough to realize that he would have to take his old self with him wherever he went, and that he might better fight things out where he stood. Men of his sort yearn constantly for the future, not realizing that in its truest sense the present *is* the future.

Only in rare instances will the deserter accept the entire responsibility for his act. To try to

* All names of deserters given throughout the text are pseudonyms.

BROKEN HOMES

find justification for doing what we want to do is characteristic of human beings, and the deserter is no exception. He attempts to "rationalize" his conduct and so regain his sense of self-approval and well-being by finding excuses and justifications in the conduct of others. Even when the fault is all his, he usually succeeds in making himself believe that his wife is more to blame than he for his having left home.* The social worker who attempts to deal with the situation the deserter creates should know this attitude in advance and be prepared, through some simple rule-of-thumb psychology, to attack the obsession and bring him, first of all, to see and face squarely his own responsibility.

Many blanket theories have been developed to explain desertion—that it is due to economic pressure; that it is the result of bad housekeeping; that its causes can all be reduced to sex incompatibility. All these factors undoubt-

---

*For an excellent discussion of the process of rationalization see The Psychology of Insanity, Bernard Hart, Cambridge University Press, 1914.

WHY DO MEN DESERT THEIR FAMILIES?

edly have their bearing on the problem, but there is no one cause or group of causes underlying breakdowns in family morale. The ratio of desertions has been observed to decrease rather than to increase in "hard times";* moreover, it is a matter of common observation that not all slovenly and incompetent wives are deserted, and that many married couples in all walks of life whose sex relationships are unsatisfactory, nevertheless maintain the fabric of family life and support and bring up their children with an average degree of success. None of these three factors alone will serve, therefore, as a fundamental causation unit in desertion. Many statistical attempts have been made to study the causes of desertion, and to assign to each its mathematical percentage of influence. The report of a court of domestic relations gives such an analysis of over 1,500 cases, listing 25 causes, and carefully calculating the percentage of cases due to each. A summary of these

* For a thoughtful discussion of this point see Eubank, E. E.: A Study of Family Desertion. Chicago Department of Public Welfare, 1916.

BROKEN HOMES

percentages grouped under five heads is as follows:

		Percentage
1.	Distinct sex factors	39.03
2.	Alcohol and narcotic drugs	37.00
3.	Temperamental traits	15.40
4.	Economic issues	6.27
5.	Mental and physical troubles	2.30
		100.00

It would be easy to criticize the foregoing on the score of grouping. Can alcoholism and drug addiction be separated from mental and physical disorders? And how distinguish infallibly between sex factors, temperamental traits, and mental disabilities? But the main defect in such statistical studies is that they assume in each case one cause, or at least one cause sufficiently dominant to dwarf the rest; and few of the causes listed are really fundamental. The mind instinctively begins to reach back after the causes of all these causes. The social worker who made the sweeping assertion that there are two great reasons for marital discord—"selfishness in men and peevishness in women"—came a good deal nearer

WHY DO MEN DESERT THEIR FAMILIES?

to an accurate statement of fact with infinitely less trouble.

Looked at from the point of view of the social worker, desertion is itself only a symptom of some more deeply seated trouble in the family structure. The problem presented, if it could have been recognized in time, is not essentially different from what it would have been before the man's departure. Without attempting, therefore, any statistical analysis of the causes of desertion, we may nevertheless be able to examine one by one a number of possible *contributory factors* in marital unhappiness and therefore in desertion. No attempt will be made in the list that follows to distinguish between primary and secondary causes, nor to arrange them in any order of importance. An effort to get from case workers lists so arranged resulted only in confusion, each person emphasizing a different set of factors. The groupings here given, therefore, are no more than a placing of the more obviously related factors together and a leading from past history up to the present.

Considering first the personal as distinguished

from the community factors in desertion, these may be listed as follows:

CONTRIBUTORY FACTORS IN THE MAN AND WOMAN

1. Actual Mental Deficiency.—Character weaknesses such as were spoken of earlier in this chapter grade down by degrees into real mental defect or disorder, and not even the psychiatrist can always draw the line.

A physician connected with the Municipal Court in Boston gives as his opinion that while the percentage of actually insane or feebleminded among deserters is no higher than among other offenders they are extremely likely to present some of the phenomena of psychopathic personality. Such people have to be studied by the social worker and the psychiatrist, and not from the behavior side only, but with a view to discovering what sort of equipment for life was handed down to them from their family stock.

The plan for the future of a fifteen-year-old boy which was made by a society for family social work was markedly modified when it was discovered that not only his

WHY DO MEN DESERT THEIR FAMILIES?

father but his grandfather had been a man of violent and abusive temper, who drank habitually and neglected his family obligations. With this sort of heredity and an ineffective mother, whom he was accustomed to seeing treated with abuse and disrespect, it was felt important to remove the boy, who showed some promise, to surroundings where he could be under firm discipline and learn decent standards of family life.

Feeble-mindedness, closely connected as it usually is with industrial inefficiency in the man, bad housekeeping in the woman, and lack of self-control in both, is of course a potent factor in non-support and probably also in desertion.

2. Faults in Early Training.—To low ideals of home life and of personal obligation, which were imbibed in youth, can be traced much family irresponsibility. It is by no means the rule, however, for children always to follow in the footsteps of weak or vicious parents; and it is the experience of social workers that such children, taught by observation to avoid the faults seen in their own homes, often make good parents themselves. Perhaps even more insidious in its effect on later marital history is

BROKEN HOMES

the home in which no self-control is learned. The so-called "good homes" in which children are exposed to petting, coddling, and overindulgence—and these homes are not confined to the wealthy—produce adults who do not stand up to their responsibilities. A probation officer in Philadelphia tells of the mother of a young deserter who could not account for her son's delinquency. "He *ought* to be a good boy," she complained; "I carried him up to bed myself every night till he was eleven years old."

3. Differences in Background.—Even though both man and wife come from good homes, if those homes are widely different in standards and in cultural background strains may develop in later life between the couple. Differences in race, religion and age are recognized as having a causative relation to desertion. Miss Brandt[*] found that, in about 28 per cent of the cases where these facts were ascertained, the husband and wife were of different nationality. "In the

[*] Brandt, Lilian: Family Desertion. The Charity Organization Society of New York City, 1905.

WHY DO MEN DESERT THEIR FAMILIES?

general population of the United States in 1900 only 8.5 per cent was of mixed parentage, and for New York City the proportion was less than 13 per cent. . . . A difference in nationality was more than twice as frequent among the cases of desertion as among the general population of the city where it is most common." Miss Brandt's figures for difference of religion are less significant, but it existed in 19 per cent of the total number of cases for which information on this point was available. In 27 per cent of the families where age-facts were learned, there were differences of over six years between the two; in 15 per cent the woman was older than the man.

Other differences which should find mention under this heading are those that arise when the environment is changed by immigration. The man who precedes his wife by many years in coming to America has often outgrown her when she finally joins him, even if he has formed no other family ties. The handicap is not wholly overcome when the couple come to this country together, for the much greater oppor-

BROKEN HOMES

tunities of the man to learn American ways may drive a wedge between him and his wife. On the other hand it is a popular saying, particularly among young Italian immigrants, that girls who have been in America too long do not make good wives, that when a man wants to marry he had better send for a girl from the old country; and these marriages seem on the whole to turn out well.

4. Wrong Basis of Marriage.—Included here should be hasty marriages, mercenary marriages, marriages entered into unwillingly after pregnancy had occurred, as well as marriages where coercion was a factor for other reasons.*

When there have been sex relations before marriage, unless the custom of the community sanctions such intimacy, there are likely to develop jealousies, quarrels, and ill feeling. "He do be always castin' it up at me, but sure, 'twas himself was to blame" is one version of the age-old story.

* For a fuller discussion of forced marriages, see p. 92 sq.

WHY DO MEN DESERT THEIR FAMILIES?

There should also be included here those irregular unions called "common law marriages," which are still permitted in many of our states. The protection supposed to be afforded to the woman by this institution is mainly fictitious, as it is practically impossible to secure conviction for bigamy if one of the marriages was of the common law variety. A common law husband who deserts, even if he admits his wife's legal claim upon him, does not feel morally bound; and this fact undoubtedly plays its part in the causation of such desertions.[*]

5. Lack of Education.—More is included under this title than scanty "book-learning." Not only the morally undisciplined child but the mentally undisciplined youth is handicapped as spouse and parent. Ignorance of the physical and spiritual bases of married life is a potent cause of desertion. So also is a limited industrial equipment. Irregular school attendance, early "working papers," a dead-end job with no educational possibilities

---

[*] See also p. 98.

BROKEN HOMES

in it—these form a frequent background for later unsuccess in life and in marriage.

There seemed at first no good explanation for the desertion of Alfred West. Both his record and his wife's were good, and their mutual fondness for the children seemed a strong bond. They constantly bickered, however, over the small income Alfred was able to earn, and his wife and her relatives "looked down" upon him as being lower than they in the social scale. Inquiry into past history showed that he had grown up in a southern community where there were no facilities for education, and that he could not even read and write until after his marriage. Although of average capacity, he was restricted by his early lack of training in his choice of a job; and the mortification and sense of inferiority which his wife fostered led to discouragement and indifference, which ended in desertion. A thorough understanding of the two backgrounds involved enabled a social worker to effect a real reconciliation, with the woman's eyes opened to her ungenerous behavior and the man taking steps to improve his education in a night school.

6. Occupational Faults.—Closely allied to the foregoing, and in some respects growing out of it, are the shortcomings on the employment side that contribute to marital instability. Most of these can be referred back to lack of education or opportunity in youth, or to defects of char-

WHY DO MEN DESERT THEIR FAMILIES?

acter. Laziness, incompetence, lack of skill in any trade, lack of application, or, on the other hand, the possession by a man with no business "stake" in the community of a trade at which he can work wherever he takes a fancy to go, or of a trade which is seasonal and shifting—all these have a direct relation to desertion.

The wife's competence and willingness to earn often seems to have a causal connection with the man's failure as "provider."*

Corresponding to and complementing the man's industrial defects, and springing from the same causes, is the woman's failure in the business of being a housewife. The wife's laziness, incompetence, lack of interest, and lack of skill and knowledge create, as one case worker puts it, "the sort of home that tends to get itself deserted." These faults of the wife are responsible for as many desertions, probably, as are the faults of the husband. When the man and the wife are both industrial failures we get the extremity of family breakdown to be found in records of "chronic non-support" cases.

* See also p. 154.

BROKEN HOMES

7. Wanderlust.—As a cause of family desertion this has probably been overestimated. Some item of this sort appears in every list of causes of desertion which has ever been compiled, and there are more or less exceptional cases in which it probably plays a part. The boy who becomes a vagabond in childhood and early takes to the road does not, however, seem to be a marrying man; and the instances from case work in which it is clear that the thirst for adventure was at the bottom of desertion are rare. The man whose line of work before marriage led him from place to place seems, in fact, hardly to contribute his quota to the ranks of wife-deserters, and it is unusual to find sailors or other wanderers from force of circumstance figuring among them.

8. Money Troubles.—As has already been said, it is impossible to show any direct relation between small incomes and desertion. The connection between low wage and non-support is of course a great deal closer. The inadequate income unquestionably acts indirectly to break

WHY DO MEN DESERT THEIR FAMILIES?

down family morale in much the same way as does lowered physical vitality.

But marital discord that springs from the *handling* of the family finances is another matter, and it recurs regularly in the history of what went on prior to desertion. One deserter, traced to a southern city, returned voluntarily and begged the assistance of the social worker interested to reform his wife's spending habits. "I made good money and I never opened my pay envelope on her," said he, "but the week's wages was always gone by Thursday." Many men, however, who make a boast of turning over unbroken pay envelopes to their wives borrow back so much in daily advances that their net contribution is only a fraction of their wages.

Some desertions brought about by financial difficulties are not, strictly speaking, marital problems at all. Debts resulting from his own extravagance or dishonesty may cause a man to leave home to escape prosecution or disgrace. One such man kept in touch with his family, sending money at irregular intervals for some years, but always moving on to another place before he could be found. It proved impossible to get in communication with him, and finally he stopped writing and disappeared.

9. Ill Health: Physical Debility.—All social workers agree that physical condition plays a part, though usually only indirectly and secondarily, in causing desertion. In the man, it may lower his vitality, cause irregular work, and superinduce a condition of despondency and readiness to give in. In the woman, it brings about careless housekeeping, loss of attractiveness, and disinclination to marital intercourse—all factors which contribute directly to desertion. Continued ill health of the wife brings burdens, financial and other, which may help through discouragement to break down the husband's morale.

There should be included here some consideration of one of the most puzzling types of abandonment—the "pregnancy desertion." Attempts have been made to explain it on the ground of the instinctive aversion of the male sex for domestic crises. But the impulse that

WHY DO MEN DESERT THEIR FAMILIES?

causes the prosperous householder to move to his club when house-cleaning time arrives will hardly serve to explain such a custom, and as a matter of fact other domestic crises, such as illnesses of the children, do not have any such effect upon the man who habitually absents himself from home before the birth of each child. Other possible reasons for it are the well-known irritability and "difficulty" of women in this condition, and their aversion to sexual intercourse. Some pregnancy deserters take the step in the hope that their wives will bring about an abortion; but this is a modern and sophisticated development and the institution of "pregnancy desertion" is one of undoubted antiquity. Its prevalence among certain European immigrants would almost point to its being a racial tradition. Ethnologists who have studied strange marriage customs, such as the "couvade," ought to turn their attention to discovering the causes of this other and socially more important marital vagary.

10. Temperamental Incompatibility.—It is difficult to catalogue and appraise the causal factors in desertion that lie in personality. They are closely related to differences in background and are intimately involved with the sex relations of the pair. We cannot, however, admit that they are identical with the latter, as some students of the subject claim; or that the only incompatibility in marriage is sex incompatibility. Indeed, two people may be so incompatible as to find in sex their only common ground.

The commonest of these temperamental differences center about standards of right and wrong or proper and improper conduct. Especially is this manifested in the bringing up of the children. Extreme self-righteousness on the part of one or the other, nagging and petty criticism, unreasonable jealousy, "sulking spells," violent quarrels, are some of its manifestations. The idea of *possession* exercised by either of the couple, and especially a tendency to dominate or try to control on the part of the woman, may be a causal factor in desertion. The lack of a saving sense of humor in one or both is often a complicating factor. These comparatively

WHY DO MEN DESERT THEIR FAMILIES?

minor differences take on a serious complexion in the minds of the couple; and it is surprising how often a deserting man will give promptly and with every appearance of feeling justified some cause for his desertion which falls clearly under this head. "People forgive each other the big things; it's the little things they can't forgive."

11. Sex Incompatibility.—There comes under this heading a wide range of causative factors which play an important part in marital discord. Some of them are better understood by the social worker than was formerly the case; but many of them are obscure even to the practitioner of mental medicine, to whom their results come daily. Distasteful as the task may be, the social worker should familiarize herself, through reading or through instruction by a qualified physician, in the commoner forms of these maladjustments. This is not urged because it is part of the social worker's task to make detailed inquiry into such matters or to pass judgment upon them, but because they

BROKEN HOMES

often clamor for attention and need to be recognized by the first responsible person to whose notice they are brought. Unless she knows, for instance, what constitutes excess in sex relations, a worker may misunderstand the situation described to her and condemn a man for being a selfish brute, when the trouble is really sexual anæsthesia in the wife. It is well known that this single cause operates disastrously to disrupt many marriages or else to render them insupportable. The warning should be added, however—and it cannot be added too emphatically—that the social worker must scrupulously refrain from making diagnoses in these cases, even tentatively; she must refer such data as come to her either to the general practitioner or to the psychiatrist, selecting one or the other as the symptoms presented may indicate.

Less well understood by the lay worker are actual maladjustments, both physical and mental (or spiritual), which prevent the complete satisfaction of one or both. Some of these are curable by medical care, others by instruction and education. This instruction should be

WHY DO MEN DESERT THEIR FAMILIES?

given, needless to say, by the physician and not by the case worker. If uncorrected such maladjustments are apt to result in marital shipwreck.

No attempt can be made here to discuss actual sex perversions in their relation to desertion. Their effect is obvious; and the social worker should be sufficiently well informed, not only from a few standard books on the subject,* but from a knowledge of the phrases which are used in the tenements, to understand them, so that significant symptoms are not overlooked. So intimately are sex difficulties connected with the neuroses that the lay social worker should consult the psychiatrist freely wherever one is available, before attempting to deal with them.

12. Vicious Habits.—Sexual immorality, through its degenerative effect on personality and the lowered ideals of marriage it induces, has a real effect in bringing about desertion. The "other

*Two books may be suggested: Forel on The Sexual Question and Havelock Ellis on Sex in Relation to Society (Vol. VI of Studies in the Psychology of Sex).

BROKEN HOMES

man" and the "other woman" type of desertion, however, is often itself only a consequence of a previously existing state of temperamental or sexual incompatibility. If these underlying causes can be attacked and changed such a desertion may be "repairable."

A young man deserted his wife and three children and eloped with an eighteen-year-old girl who had made his acquaintance in a street car flirtation. He had been "an obedient boy with good principles," and his later record showed steadiness and ability; but he and his wife had been drifting apart—their marital relations had not been "quite the same" as formerly. Arrested and brought back, he did not impute any blame to her, however, but said he "must have been crazy." In spite of the circumstances, the judge decided to give him six months in the penitentiary; and a man visitor from the family social agency interested began at once to try to secure an influence over him. On his release the couple again went to housekeeping. The wife had been cautioned on how to receive him; but things went badly at first, and the man began again insisting that they were mismated. (He "had the other girl still considerably on his conscience and heart.") Tangles continually arose which the society's visitor was hard put to it to straighten out. Once the wife found a letter from the girl; but finally, after the charity organization society in the city where he had left the girl reported that she was doing well and not

WHY DO MEN DESERT THEIR FAMILIES?

breaking her heart about him, the man decided to "cut out" the correspondence. A little later the girl eliminated herself by marrying. A year after the reconciliation the wife told the friendly visitor that the trouble was gone between them, and "it was just like a new life." For another year efforts were continued to strengthen the attachment and make the home more attractive, at the end of which time it was felt that the home was stable enough to need no further supervision.

For reasons of convenience we may include here the causal relations between venereal disease and desertion. In so far as syphilis brings about mental and physical deterioration, the relation between the two is obvious. The presence of the disease in the man, if known to his wife, may lead her to sever relations with him in self-protection, and this severance, in turn, may lead ultimately to desertion or complete separation. Often separation is desirable, but the syphilitic who is on the whole a good family man raises some of the most difficult questions with which the social worker has to deal. Whether to try to force him out of the home and thus make an unwilling deserter; whether to violate the diagnosis given in confidence by passing it on to the wife for her protection—these are only two of the puzzles that may arise.

The relation of alcoholism to non-support and desertion is too well known to require discussion. The causative relation between alcohol and desertion is so direct that it probably ought not to be included under contributory causes at all. As it is an active poison to the cells of the nervous system, it may bring about deteriorations of mind and character that are directly to blame for such anti-social acts as desertion. The same is true in less degree of the use of narcotics; though drug habits are far less common in connection with desertion than alcoholism. What relation drugs and alcohol will hold to desertion after July 1, 1919, remains to be seen. Alcoholism in the woman is, however, a real contributory factor, and one frequently met with. The experience of social workers leads them to believe that alcohol is more devastating in its effects on character with women than with men, and that there is less hope of a cure. The great majority of so-called "justifiable deserters" are the husbands of alcoholic women.

WHY DO MEN DESERT THEIR FAMILIES?

Gambling in its effect on family income will be discussed in connection with non-support, to which it bears a much more direct relation than to desertion. In its degenerative effect upon character it may have, however, a real causal relation to the latter.

The habit of desertion itself is a degenerative one, not only upon the deserter but upon his home. The "intermittent husband" often weakens and demoralizes his wife in almost the same ratio as his own progress down-hill.

CONTRIBUTORY FACTORS IN THE COMMUNITY

1. Interference of Relatives.—The tendency of relatives to take sides against their "in-laws" is a matter of everyone's observation. It is frequently found as a serious factor in desertion. Many case stories which will be used in the following chapters to illustrate other points show also the harmful interference of relatives in what might otherwise have been a fairly stable home. Relatives can be a factor in marital discord without actively interfering. One high-tempered young couple formed what amounted to a habit of frequent quarrels and temporary separations simply because the parents of both stood ready to take them back whenever they chose to live apart. Relatives within the home as well as outside it may exercise an unfortunate influence on marital relations. The desertion of a middle-aged man who married a widow was found to be directly caused by the antagonism which grew up between him and his grown step-children.

2. Racial Attitude toward Marriage.—The racial factor is important in desertion. Not only the individual's own background, but the attitude of the people whence he sprang toward the sanctity of marriage, toward the position of women, and toward the importance of restraint in sexual relations, will have an effect upon the desertion rate of a given racial group. A study was recently made of 480 deserters known to the New York Charity Organization Society in 1916-17 whose nationality was given. The results in percentage form are given for what they may be worth, compared with the same percentage in

WHY DO MEN DESERT THEIR FAMILIES?

2,987 families of known nationalities which were under care for all causes during the same year.

NATIONALITY OR RACE

Race or place of birth	Per cent among 480 deserters	Per cent among 2,987 families under care for all causes
United States—white	30.6	29.7
" —colored	11.2	5.6
Irish	9.7	14.7
Other British	5.0	4.7
German	6.2	6.2
Italian	20.2	28.0
Austrian	5.5	4.8
Russian	2.8	1.0
Polish	3.3	1.2
Other	5.5	4.1
	100.0	100.0

3. Community Standards.—It cannot be too emphatically stated that any tendency in the community to belittle or ridicule the estate of matrimony has a definite cumulative effect on desertion. The "when a man's married" series in the comic supplements, certain comic films

BROKEN HOMES

in the moving picture shows, the form of drama popularly called "bedroom farce" are examples of these destructive forces. Most of the people who laugh at them accept them as a humorous formula and are not seriously affected by them; but their educational effect on young people is bound to be bad and false to the last degree. In so far as they overemphasize romantic love and disparage conjugal love, the theater and the popular press do this generation great disservice.

Another way in which the community may affect the popular conception of marriage is in the administration of civil marriage. Lack of care in enforcing the laws and lack of gravity in performing the ceremonies may have a decided reaction on respect for those laws and for the institution itself. Similarly, the administration of divorce laws may affect the popular conception of marriage. One entire neighborhood condoned the situation in which a deserted wife immediately went to live with another man, on the ground that "if they had been rich, they could have got a divorce."

WHY DO MEN DESERT THEIR FAMILIES?

4. Lack of Proper Recreation.—This may seem a subject to be discussed under personal factors; but proper recreation, after all, depends in large measure upon what the community provides or makes available. The American tendency for the man to get his recreation apart from his family, in saloons and social clubs, is responsible for many family maladjustments. Any change in family habits of recreation which means that the man and wife enjoy fewer things together is a danger signal the seriousness of which is not always appreciated. Social workers are inclined to undervalue not only the influence of faulty recreation as a factor in family breakdown, but also the possibilities of good recreation as an aid in family reconstruction.

5. Influence of Companions.—As a factor in desertion this is closely connected with the two just discussed. Neighborhood standards, as they affect individuals, are apt to be transmitted through the small group that stands nearest, and a man's companions have the freest opportunity to influence him during their common periods of recreation. The influence of companions is not often met as a force deliberately exerted to bring about desertion; but, on the other hand, a man's own mental contrast between his condition and that of his unmarried companions often plays a definite part in his decision to desert, if he has begun to yearn for freedom. The influence of companions is particularly connected with the "wanderlust" type of desertion.

6. Expectation of Charitable Relief.—It used to be held that many men who would otherwise remain at home and support, might be encouraged to desert if they had reason to believe that their wives and families would be cared for in their absence. This was no doubt often the case before social workers had learned to discriminate in treatment between deserted wives and widows, or to press with vigor the search for deserting men. At present, it is the experience of social workers that few men deliberately reckon upon transferring the burden

WHY DO MEN DESERT THEIR FAMILIES?

of their family's support to others, or are induced by these considerations to leave.*

In trying to determine the cause for any given desertion it is well to keep in mind from the beginning that there is probably more than one, and that the obvious causes that first appear are almost certain themselves to be the effects of more deeply underlying causes. A young vaudeville actor of Italian parentage married a Jewish girl, a cabaret singer, and took her home to live with his parents. Was his subsequent desertion to be ascribed to difference in nationality and religion, to interference of relatives, to irregular and unsettling occupation, or to a combination of all three? Would all marriages so handicapped turn out as badly? If not, what further factors entered to lower the threshold of resistance to disintegration in this particular case?

This last question is after all the most important one of the foregoing series. It is one which the social case worker must never be content to leave unanswered.

* See p. 70 sq. for a discussion of collusive desertion.

III

CHANGES OF EMPHASIS IN TREATMENT

UNCONSCIOUSLY and imperceptibly, the point of view about the treatment of desertion has been changing during the past fifteen years. The case worker's attention used to be focussed on the danger of increasing the desertion rate by a policy of too sympathetic care for deserters' families. Little study was made of individual causes, and in so far as there was a general policy of treatment it was to insist, wherever a desertion law existed, that the deserted wife go at once to court and institute proceedings against her husband. He was often not seen by the social worker until he appeared in court. The policy toward the family meantime was to reduce its size by commitment of the children until their mother could support herself unaided; or, if relief was given, to give smaller amounts than to a widow or the wife

CHANGES OF EMPHASIS IN TREATMENT

of a man in hospital. As soon as the man had been placed under court order or had returned home, old records generally show that the social worker's efforts were relaxed, and often the final entry is, "Case closed—family self-supporting."

There were excellent reasons underlying much of the practice. Few laws were at that time in existence or at all adequately enforced, and any man who desired was at liberty, so far as the community was concerned, to walk off and leave his family at any time. The multiplicity of sources of relief in the large communities and the absence of anything resembling investigation constituted almost an invitation to men to desert. It did not occur to the charitable public to draw any line between the widow and the deserted wife, or indeed to inquire which of these two a woman was, so long as she was a good mother and "seemed worthy." No wonder that the pioneering social agencies, busy forging tools out of the very ore, took a rigid stand on such a question of social policy as this. Although their deterrents failed to eradicate the evil of desertion or indeed to touch its sources, there is little doubt that they did lessen its volume by creating a wholesome respect for the power of the law in the mind of the would-be deserter and by fostering in his wife a disposition to stand up for her rights. The more lenient and more constructive policies now in force have been made possible in part by these changes of attitude. The very fact that the collusive desertion, once fairly common, is now seldom met with, illustrates the salutary effects of the earlier methods of treatment.

But the fact remains that no marked change has been seen in the desertion rate, that successive desertions have not been prevented in individual cases. Hardly any statistical figure in the work of family social agencies shows so little fluctuation from year to year and between different cities, as the percentage of deserted families. It generally forms from ten to fifteen per cent of the work of any such society.

Gradually, therefore, the repressive features of the earlier treatment have been abandoned, and there has come about a realization of the complexity of causes that bring about family

CHANGES OF EMPHASIS IN TREATMENT

breakdowns. In particular, the relation of sex maladjustments to failure in marriage have received the serious attention of the social worker. On the question of court intervention there has been almost a right-about face; the best social practitioners now say, unhesitatingly and unequivocally, that they take cases into court only as a matter of last resort, after case work methods have been tried and have failed. In no other case where court action is undertaken by one individual against another does the relation between them remain unchanged. One could not conceive of a business partnership failing to be annulled by one partner who brought suit against another; yet we expect the marriage relation to survive this. As a matter of fact, such is its vitality that it often does. But many times the result of court action is only to deaden once and for all the tiny spark from which marital happiness might have been rekindled. As long as it survives, both man and wife feel in their inmost hearts that, no matter what his offense, to "take him to court" is treason against the intangible bonds that still hold between

BROKEN HOMES

them. No matter how far apart they have drifted, or how unforgivable has been the deserter's offense, something irrevocable does happen to the fabric of marriage, a few poor shreds of which may still exist between the two, when his wife appears in a court of law to make complaint against him. It is an instinctive realization that she is abandoning hope which underlies many a woman's reluctance to "take a stand against her husband." Many social workers (including some probation officers and court workers) now feel that such a stand should be urged only in the full conviction that the protection of the woman and children demands it, and that there is nothing else to be done.

This must not, however, be interpreted as a criticism of the laws concerning desertion or of the courts which administer them. If they were not there in the background, ready to be taken advantage of when all else fails, the social worker's hands would be tied, and the possibility of a rich and flexible treatment of desertion problems would be lost to her. It is precisely because they had no such recourse that the case

CHANGES OF EMPHASIS IN TREATMENT

workers of an earlier day had to adopt a policy which now seems rigid. It is because they were instrumental in securing better laws and specialized courts that the latter day social worker can push forward her own technique of dealing with homes that are disintegrating.

Another great change in emphasis has been upon the question of interviewing the man, and of being sure that his side, or what he thinks is his side, has been thoroughly understood. Social workers are under conviction of sin in the matter of dealing too exclusively with the woman of the family; in desertion cases it is more than desirable, it is vitally necessary to have dealings with the man. Many social workers feel that, at all events with a first desertion, they would rather take the risk of having the man vanish a second time after having been found, than have him arrested before an attempt to talk the matter out with him. More stringent measures, they believe, can be resorted to later—but the man must first be convinced that he will be listened to patiently and with the intent to deal fairly. The case worker knows that the

BROKEN HOMES

power of the human mind to "rationalize" anti-social conduct is infinite; and that, besides the few "justifiable deserters," there are many who have succeeded in convincing themselves that their action is warrantable. A deserter who could allege nothing else against his wife, averred that he had placed under the bed two matches, crossed, and a week later found them in the same position, proving his contention that she was slovenly and did not keep the rooms clean.

The man who, aided by a sore conscience, has worked himself into such a state of mind as this must be permitted to talk himself out before he can be made to see the true state of affairs. In the minds of both man and woman there is likely to be found a superstructure of suspicion, jealousy, misinterpretation and distrust, built upon the basic fact of their incompatibility, which has to be pulled down before the true causes can be probed. To arrest a man in this state of mind is in his eyes simply to "take sides" against him. Eventually he may have to be arrested, but, in the case worker's experience, the chances of success are ten to

CHANGES OF EMPHASIS IN TREATMENT

one if the man can be induced to take some voluntary step toward reconciliation without the intervention of the law. In many instances a real interview with the man, while not exonerating him, would have thrown new light on the woman's statements.

A family social work society writes: A young woman with her mother and little boy were referred for aid by a medical social department because her husband had deserted and she was unable to work. The doctors feared that her breakdown would result in insanity, so they asked that her wishes be respected in not seeing the man's family. She recovered, but it was later found that her husband, while not doing all that he might for her, had been living at home a good deal of the time and did not know that his family was in receipt of aid.

Some years ago a charity organization society, which maintained a special bureau for treatment of desertion cases, was asked by a Mrs. Clara Williams to help her find her husband, John, who had left her some years previously and was living with another woman, so that she might force him to contribute to the support of herself and her two children. Mrs. Williams was a motherly appearing person who kept a clean, neat home, and seemed to take excellent care of her children. She was voluble concerning her husband's misdeeds and very bitter toward him, which seemed only natural. The fact of the other household was corroborated from other

BROKEN HOMES

sources, and Mr. Williams' work references indicated that he had been quarrelsome and difficult for his employers to get along with, although a competent workman. The problem seemed to the desertion agent a perfectly clear and uncomplicated one and he proceeded to handle it according to the formula. Some very clever detective work followed, in the course of which the man was traced from one suburban city to another, and his present place of employment found in the city where his wife lived, although he lived just across the border of another state. The warrant was served upon the man as he stepped from the train on his way to work, and he appeared in the domestic relations court. He did not deny the desertion but made some attempt to bring counter charges against his wife. When questioned about his present mode of living he became silent and refused to testify further. He was placed under bond, which was furnished by the relatives of the woman with whom he was living, to pay his wife $6.00 a week. No probation was thought necessary and the case was closed, both the court and the charity organization society crediting themselves with a case successfully handled and terminated.

About a year later Mrs. Williams again applied, stating that her husband's bond had lapsed, his payment had ceased, and that she had no knowledge of his whereabouts. Although her home and children were still immaculate she failed to satisfy the social worker who this time visited her home with the plausible story which she had told before. The children's health was not good and they seemed unnaturally repressed and unhappy. Ugly

CHANGES OF EMPHASIS IN TREATMENT

reports that Mrs. Williams drank came to the society. The school teacher deplored the effect which the morbid nature of Mrs. Williams was having on her youngest child—a daughter just entering adolescence. The son, a boy a little older, was listless and unsatisfactory at his work, and defiant and secretive toward any attempt to get to know him better. He spent many nights away from home and was evidently not on good terms with his mother. As soon as Mrs. Williams saw that real information was desired she began indulging in fits of rage in which she displayed such an exaggerated ego as to cause some doubts as to her mentality. Baffled at every turn the case worker decided to interview the man, if possible, to see if through him any clue to the situation might be gained. The first step was to gain the confidence of a former fellow-workman and friend of his who now maintained his own small shop. This was done after several visits, the deserting husband consenting to an evening meeting in his friend's shop.

A most illuminating interview followed. Mr. Williams was found to be an intelligent though melancholy and self-centered man. The couple had married somewhat late in life, it being Mrs. Williams' second marriage. She had been strongly influenced by her mother to marry him and had never had any real affection for him. It became very evident from his story that the strongly developed egotism of both the husband and wife had made a real marriage impossible between them, and the visitor became convinced of the genuineness of Mr. Williams' protestations that he endured the constant

BROKEN HOMES

abuse and ill-treatment of his wife as long as it had been possible to do so. As her drinking habits took more hold upon her and he had realized that the break was coming he had endeavored to place the children in homes, and had once had his wife taken into court. There her plausible story and good appearance resulted in the case being dismissed with a reprimand to the husband. He then left home, but continued to send her money at intervals, although as he got older he was able to earn less at his trade. Socialism was his religion, and it was his preaching of this doctrine in season and out to his fellow workmen which had earned him the ill-will of his employers. He defended his present mode of living, vigorously putting up a strong argument that it was a real marriage, whereas the other had only been a sham. He spoke in terms of affection of the woman who was giving him the only real home he had ever known, and only wished that the state of public opinion would permit his taking his young daughter into his home. The boy, he realized, had grown entirely away from him and they could never mean anything to each other. It was his habit to make frequent trips back to the region where his family lived in order that he might stand on the corner and watch his children go by. He gave readily much information about his own and his wife's past connections, including the addresses of many of her relatives whose existence she had denied, and he successfully proved that her claims as to his lapsed payments were false by producing the entire series of post office receipts covering his remittances to

CHANGES OF EMPHASIS IN TREATMENT

her and extending down to the very week of the interview.*

There have been striking changes not only in the treatment of the deserter but in that of his family. Writing in 1910, Miss Breed† deprecates the habit of fostering the deserter's "easy-going conviction that his family will get along somehow without him" by giving relief. She approves offering full support in an institution, but is reluctant to recommend any form of aid in the home, even from relatives. It is better, she feels, to give entire support to some of the children in foster homes, leaving the mother only those she can care for.

Much can be said for even so stringent a policy as this. An unstable home, with a worthless father an intermittent member of the household, is as bad an environment as children can have—its very fluctuations making for nervous

* Adapted from the writer's article on "Desertion and Non-Support in Family Case Work," *The Annals of the Academy of Political and Social Science*, May, 1918, p. 98.

† Breed, Mary: Eleventh New York State Conference, 1910, p. 76.

BROKEN HOMES

instability and a wrong point of view later on. There is a possibility that other would-be deserters may be deterred by temporarily breaking up the home, and that an occasional absconding father may be brought back. But the fact remains that social workers have, in practice, departed far from this point of view. Out of more than twenty-five case workers of experience who were interviewed or written to in preparation for this book, only one believed there had not been a decided change toward a policy of more liberal relief.

One district secretary told of a woman who had more than once taken back a disreputable husband whom she always professed to dislike. Aid was given sparingly and intermittently during his absences; but finally the woman in a burst of frankness told the secretary that she had never felt confident the society would stand behind her. Each time the man came back with money in his hand, she cheated herself into believing that he meant "a new leaf." A budget was worked out with her, and a promise given of an adequate income as long as she kept her husband away. She has faithfully kept her side of the bargain for over three years.

The extension in many states of "state aid to

CHANGES OF EMPHASIS IN TREATMENT

mothers" to cover deserted wives is an indication of this changed view. In most states, however, some safeguards are set up; the wife must take out a warrant, and a given number of years must elapse during which the man shall not have been heard from, before state aid can be granted to the wife.

Finally, it is more clearly recognized than formerly that the time to "close the case" is not just after the man's return.

A case supervisor speaks of "the strong temptation to close our records as soon as relief becomes unnecessary. The man's return to the family is often the critical point at which there is need of skilful and sympathetic friendship. These cases cry out for continued treatment. We need to think more humanely about all the unsettling elements in our urban civilization and to see that all the nice individual adjustments that as case workers we can make are made. If the man's work gives him no opportunity for self-expression, what attempt are we making to give him such opportunities outside his work, to connect him with a trade union, with clubs and with fraternities? How much are we thinking about cures for inebriates, psychoanalysis, vocational guidance, recreation?"

Briefly, then, changes in the social worker's attitude toward treatment have meant less

BROKEN HOMES

emphasis on punitive and repressive measures, more consideration of the man's point of view, less tendency to press court action, at least in the beginning, fewer commitments of children, a more liberal relief policy (partly as a preventive of "forced reconciliations"), and lastly, longer supervision after the man has resumed support of his family.

IV

FINDING THE DESERTING HUSBAND

A FEW years ago a young Jewish woman reported to the National Desertion Bureau* that her husband had left her and their children.

The couple had never got on well, and the man seemed to have been a melancholy and impractical fellow. The usual methods of the Bureau brought no results in finding the missing husband. Then the wife was more carefully questioned, and urged to tell all that she could recall or had heard about her husband's early life, his tastes and peculiarities. Among other things the Bureau learned that the man's father had died in America years ago, having come here to make a home for the family left behind in Russia. The boy had grown up in ignorance of the place of his father's death and burial, and, as the eldest son, he felt it his duty to find his father's grave. Filled with this idea he came to America as soon as he was

* The National Desertion Bureau, 356 Second Avenue, New York, acts in a legal advisory capacity to Jewish organizations in matters of domestic relations; it also seeks out Jewish family deserters, with a view to assuring their rehabilitation or, failing this, their punishment.

BROKEN HOMES

grown and landed in New York, but his few poor clues availed him little against the difficulties of poverty and a new and complex environment. In the end he gave up the search, married, and settled down on the east side. After the sudden quarrel which led to his leaving home, his wife thought it possible that his old obsession might have reawakened. The Bureau, supplied with the clues in question, had little difficulty in discovering the father's burial place in St. Louis; and the cemetery authorities promised to send word if the missing husband should appear. Sure enough, a short time afterward he arrived, and, after visiting the grave, returned, not unwillingly, and took up his family duties again under the supervision of a probation officer.

The flexibility of method and the readiness to see and utilize new resources which are displayed in the foregoing account are great assets to the one who must institute search for a missing husband and father.

The thing that sets desertion cases apart in a class of peculiar technical difficulty for the case worker is not simply that the man is away from his family. There is no man to deal with in a widow's family, but widows' families present comparatively simple problems. The deserter, though absent, is still not only a potential but

FINDING THE DESERTING HUSBAND

also a real factor in the family situation. The plans of the family are often made with one eye to his return; he is the unseen but plainly felt obstacle to much that the social worker wants to accomplish. The children look forward to his reappearance with dread or with joy (for many deserters have a way with them, decidedly, and are welcome visitors to their children). In short, he is usually at the key point in the situation. No plan can safely be made that leaves him out, but—there's the rub!—you cannot include him at once for he is not to be reached, certainly not at the outset. The discovery of the deserter's whereabouts is not only the first but the most urgent of the problems that confront the worker who tries to deal with a deserted family. Unless he can be found the whole plan rests upon shifting sand.

A prompt and vigorous effort to find the absentee is therefore a first requisite in dealing with family desertion. Unfortunately, many case workers, having started bravely and exhausted the first crop of clues, become discouraged and fall back on the supposition that the

BROKEN HOMES

man is permanently out of the scene, and that it only remains to make plans for the family. Numberless case histories attest the unwisdom of this assumption. It is not making an extreme statement to say that, as long as the family remains under active care or until the missing man is proved to be dead, the effort to find him should not be abandoned. Mr. Carstens, in discussing this point, says:

> To carry on this search persistently is the great safeguard. It is rare when in the course of a few months the true state of affairs will not have been revealed, though it may have been quite hidden at the start.*

This is not to say that time must be spent unprofitably in going over the same ground, or that out-of-town agencies must be badgered to reinvestigate old clues. But the frame of mind that pigeonholes the whole matter as having been attended to must be shunned by the social worker, who should be always on the alert for new clues and prompt to follow them up. An example of a vigorous and persistent search for

* C. C. Carstens, Proceedings of the Fifth New York State Conference of Charities and Correction, 1904, p. 196.

FINDING THE DESERTING HUSBAND

a deserter is taken from the files of the National Desertion Bureau.*

Adolph R. deserted his wife and their six little children on September 1, 1912. He was traced to Philadelphia, but had left there the day before the tidings reached New York. Information was obtained from fellow-employes which led to the belief that he had gone to Tampa, Florida. Inquiry was directed to the rabbi in that city, but again the information was disheartening, since it disclosed the fact that once more R. had "left the day before." The rabbi telegraphed that the deserter had evidently gone to Lakewood, Florida, and that he could be found in that place. Immediately the Bureau dispatched a telegram to its representative there, only to find that R. had merely passed through Lakewood en route to Bartow, Florida. When the inquiry reached Bartow it was learned that R. had left a few days before, and that he was on his way to Memphis, Tennessee. The Jewish Charities of Memphis made investigation at the cigar factories of that city, but reported that no person bearing the name of R. or resembling him had been seen in their city. No further clue to his whereabouts could be secured.

Months later R. applied to the Jewish Charities of Louisville for transportation to New York, making an entirely false statement about his family.

This statement was telegraphed to the Bureau and no time was lost in securing a warrant. Louisville was noti-

* See p. 65, footnote.

BROKEN HOMES

fied by wire to arrest, but again a telegram came: "Adolph R. left city. Learned from Cigarmakers' Union headquarters he went to Cincinnati. Wire Joe Rapp, 1316 Walnut Street, Cincinnati Union Headquarters. Man said he was going to Cincinnati or Indianapolis. Man joined union Richmond, Va., November 19, 1911, and reports to union in all cities." The Desertion Bureau immediately telegraphed to Cincinnati and Indianapolis. The United Jewish Charities of Cincinnati working together with the labor union lost little time in effecting his arrest.

Many theories about family desertion have suffered a change in recent years. One of these relates to the "collusive desertion." Social workers in training used formerly to be taught that the first place to look for the deserter was around the corner, where he could slip back into the house and partake of charitable bounty or, at the very least, keep close watch of his family and return if any serious danger threatened them. Although the collusive desertion seems to have been a frequent happening in the past, there is almost unanimous testimony from case workers at the present time that it is not common. "I don't come across an instance once a year," said one case worker.

FINDING THE DESERTING HUSBAND

Another, after searching her memory, recalled what seemed to her one instance of real collusion. A woman, pregnant and seeming to be in great destitution, applied to a family social work society in a small city for help. Careful search did not discover the man's whereabouts—he seemed to have disappeared without leaving a trace, and his wife professed ignorance. Some two weeks after this the visitor, calling late, met a man on the stairs who proved to be the missing husband. Times were hard and he was out of a job, so he had taken to the attic of their house, and had kept so strictly *incommunicado* that not only the society but the neighbors had been deceived.

Out of twenty or more case workers in different cities whose experience was sought on this point, nearly all felt that the warnings against possible collusion which used to be given to young workers no longer needed to be emphasized. Testimony in the other direction is, however, advanced by the National Desertion Bureau, which found that about 10 per cent of the applications made in 1910 to the United Hebrew Charities of New York for relief because of desertion were collusive.

It should be said, however, that one form of collusion is common to the experience of case workers—that of the wife who knows where her husband is, or has a very good idea, but does not want him to return and so keeps her knowledge to herself. "In two of our regular allowance families," writes the case supervisor of a family agency, "we discovered—one quite incidentally, one after the allowance had been discontinued for other reasons—that the wife had had reports regarding the man which we might have followed up had we known of them earlier. It could hardly be called collusion—it was mere indifference." A probation officer writes:

"At the present time we have under investigation a family where the man has been away from home for two years and his whereabouts during the last year have been known to his wife. He has been living in a suburb of the city and working steadily during that time. The woman has received adequate aid from public and private organizations. She has been content to accept that rather than notify the authorities and have her husband required to meet the responsibility. The man on his part was aware that his family was being supported, and while there was no agreement between the parties regarding it, nevertheless the arrangement apparently met with mutual approval."

To guard against this and similar omissions on the woman's part, more than one agency

FINDING THE DESERTING HUSBAND

which deals with family desertion requires the deserted wife to sign an affidavit that she has given all the information she possesses.

Although in practice the possibility of a collusive desertion is not the first and most important thing to keep in mind, it is frequent enough not to be entirely forgotten. And for yet other reasons it is well to keep a watchful eye upon the neighborhood in which the family is living for reports about the man. Often obscure impulses seem to bring him back; jealousy of the wife or a desire to show himself in a spirit of bravado, or even sometimes a fugitive affection for the children he has abandoned may cause him to appear in the neighborhood. "The deserter, like the murderer, harks back to the scene of his misdeeds" was the generalization of one district secretary.

Even when he does not appear in the flesh the deserter may seek news of his family. "One deserter was found through the Attendance Department [of the public school system] to which he wrote after a three years' absence ask-

BROKEN HOMES

ing the address of one of the children of whom he was especially fond."

There is little in the literature of the subject covering methods of discovering deserters, nor do case workers generally appear to have developed a special technique. The decided reaction against detective methods which has been apparent in the profession during later years may help to explain this fact. Most social workers feel a subconscious sense of injustice in having to do this work at all, since it is properly a function of the police. Prosecutors and police officials generally take very little interest in following up deserters, and have little idea of giving any treatment to the deserter who has been found other than arraignment and conviction. It is difficult for the probation officer or the family case worker to hold up the machinery of the law, once it has been started, and to do this long enough to find out whether some other form of treatment best suits the case. For these reasons the social worker usually prefers to do or else is forced to do the work of the

FINDING THE DESERTING HUSBAND

detective in desertion cases up to the point where arrest is in his judgment necessary.

A probation officer in D——— found that he could not work through the local police in searching for a certain deserter, because the missing man's political affiliations made them friendly to him. The probation officer knew in a general way that the man was likely to be in the city of S——— in the same state, so he secured a warrant and sent it with such slight clues as were at hand, to a probation officer of that city who was successful in the search. Avoiding the usual procedure, the warrant was served by the police in S———. "Several instances of this kind have occurred lately," writes the probation officer at D———.

The necessity of doing the detective's work raises at once the question of how far the social worker can afford to adopt the detective's methods. If reformation of the man is the end sought it would seem an axiom that he must be given from the first every reason to believe that the social worker will play fair. "We are very careful never to break a promise we have made to a man," says an agency which deals with many deserters. The same agency, as illustration of its own methods in seeking deserting

BROKEN HOMES

men, instances the case of a man who was being shielded by his sister, but was discovered by an officer who scraped acquaintance with her little boy and asked innocently, "Where's your uncle Jack now?" In another case the officer learned of a man's whereabouts through his relatives by representing himself as a lawyer's clerk calling about a legacy which had been left the man. In still another case, reported by a different agency, a man who had deserted his family was known to be receiving mail through the general delivery of another city. It was ascertained that he was writing to a woman in his home town. A letter was sent to him in care of General Delivery asking him to meet the writer (who was represented to be the young woman with whom he was corresponding). The wife was sent to that city and she and the local probation officer met the man and served the warrant.

There is, of course, something to be said in favor of the use of such methods. The protection of the weak and helpless may justify, in certain circumstances, any subterfuge. But the *detective* who arrests the criminal in ways like

FINDING THE DESERTING HUSBAND

these is seeking his punishment and nothing else. There is no thought in that case of establishing personal relations and effecting the long, slow process of reformation. When social workers use such methods it should be in the full realization that they are foregoing any future advantage of straight dealing with the man. To capture a man by a trick is to declare war on him; and, in his mind, the social worker and the policeman then stand in the same place. "I'd have him there to meet you," said a deserter's chum to a woman visitor, "if I wasn't sure, in spite of your straight talk, you'd have a bull waiting behind a tree."*

---

*This paragraph was submitted to the two agencies which furnished the illustrations. Their replies are in part as follows:

Agency A.—"Your criticism . . . is purely theoretical and has no basis in fact. The deserter is a knowing violator of the law, and while he does not welcome it, he regards his arrest as only a question of time. He is playing the game of 'hide and seek,' and he is applying every trick and subterfuge to avoid detection. He is not disturbed if he has been caught in a police trap. Our experience has been that in such cases where he has tried to outwit the police, and the police finally have 'beaten him to the game,' he compliments his captor. This is a common characteris-

BROKEN HOMES

What are some concrete suggestions, developed from the experience of case workers, as to how to proceed in searching for deserting men? A full and careful talk with the wife is the first requisite, supplemented by equally thorough interviews with any near relatives who can be reached. The case worker should be familiar with the Questionnaire on the Deserted Family in Mary E. Richmond's Social Diagnosis. A description and if possible a photograph of the man should be procured. Where several out-of-town clues are to be followed, copies of the photograph can be cheaply made, and at least one bureau for dealing with desertion cases makes this part of its routine procedure.

---

tic of the criminal, a sort of negative bravado. When the deserter is arrested, all he can hope for and expect is a fair deal."

Agency B.—"I have seen very few individuals in the course of my experience who could not be brought to see the right viewpoint if they were intelligently approached, even though the probation officer had considerable to do with their arrest. It is in my opinion not altogether important what occurs before the man's arrest but how he is treated after he comes within the jurisdiction of the probation officials."

FINDING THE DESERTING HUSBAND

If it is a first desertion, or if there is room for doubt whether an accident may have befallen the man, police and hospital records should be looked up.

A woman with four children applied to a charity organization society, saying her husband had disappeared. There was a rumor that someone had seen him fall off the dock while intoxicated, but no attempt had been made to confirm this and the family was treated as a deserted family for some months, until the man's body was found in the river and identified.

If there have been previous desertions, it is extremely important to secure their history. The reasons that moved the man once are likely to do so again, and he is apt to return to his former haunts and be seen by former friends and acquaintances.

The deserting man, unless he elopes with another woman, generally goes to some cheap lodging house or, if of foreign birth, he may seek out the quarter where those of his nationality reside and become a lodger in a family in which his native tongue is spoken. Hence, a canvass of the lodging houses—armed with a

BROKEN HOMES

photograph if possible—is a desirable first step. All of the social worker's casual acquaintance with the foreign quarters of his city comes into play in the search. If the man is in the city some "landsmann," some "paesano" has seen him, and knows where he is to be found. It may even narrow down to finding the particular house on the particular street where the immigrants from a particular village in Sicily or Galicia have their abode. The pool-rooms and saloons of the district can often be made to yield information, especially if a man visitor can canvass them. In dealing in this way with mere acquaintances of the man, it is usually not necessary for the social worker to tell who he himself is or to state the purpose of his inquiry. In talking with relatives or close friends, however, it is often best to lay all cards on the table and convince one's listener first of all that the man sought will have fair treatment and a chance to state his side of the case before any proceedings are begun against him.

Even a relative who has never been seen may sometimes be induced to act effectively.

FINDING THE DESERTING HUSBAND

A man who deserted his wife and family was reported to have gone to his brother in another city. Nothing definite was known of the brother except that he was a telephone lineman. No address could be secured through the company, but they agreed to forward a letter to this relative. He never answered; shortly, however, the deserter reappeared, having been persuaded to return voluntarily by the brother to whom the letter had been addressed.

During the war local draft boards were of the greatest assistance in finding deserting men. Election records too have been of real value in the case of men who were voters. Passports and immigration records may in some instances yield information helpful in establishing whereabouts. Where there is actually a warrant out for the man's arrest, the active co-operation of the postal authorities can sometimes be secured in furnishing return addresses on envelopes delivered to persons with whom the culprit is known to be in correspondence.

Problems of family desertion involving men in service during the war were in the main handled by the Red Cross Home Service. Before the war, private case working agencies had

BROKEN HOMES

learned that the regular Army and the Navy often seemed desirable havens to would-be family deserters. The difficulties of finding them there were great, owing to the fact that they often enlisted as single men under an assumed name. It has usually been possible to gain excellent co-operation from the military authorities if there are any clues whatever.

The desertion bureau of a family social work society learned that a deserting man had expressed a desire long before he left his family to enlist in the Army. Several letters were exchanged with the War Department, and the man was finally found to be with a company serving in the Canal Zone. As he had made misrepresentations when he enlisted, the War Department was willing to transfer him from Panama to a camp within the limits of the city where the desertion had taken place and there discharge him. This brought the absconder within the jurisdiction of the local courts and made it possible to arrest him as soon as he was outside the bounds of the camp.

It will repay the visitor to make not only a careful study of the deserting man's employment history but also to learn something about the trade he follows. A cloakmaker, for instance,

FINDING THE DESERTING HUSBAND

who deserts in New York City is likely to be found in Cleveland, for these are the two centers of the cloak branch of the garment trade. Certain seasonal occupations give the periodical deserter a great opportunity. Among these are hop picking, berry picking, and lumbering. The amusement parks near the large cities also furnish occupation for the seasonal deserter. The case worker cannot be expected to have such knowledge at his finger-tips, but he can go to people who know about the fluctuations of particular trades—to employers, union officials or fellow-workmen who may throw light on a deserter's movements. The story of Adolph R.* is an excellent illustration of the help that may be obtained from trades unions and from fellow-workmen. A family welfare bureau in a western city writes:

"In one instance a blacksmith's union published the picture of the deserting man in its official journal and asked that information regarding him be sent to the local unit here. This proved successful. In another instance a union gave us access to its books and helped us to trace

* See p. 69.

BROKEN HOMES

all the men of a given name listed there. By this means we found the man we were looking for. One man, a vaudeville performer, we traced through the *Bill Board* (a trade paper) by discovering the movements of the show with which he had been connected."

Another society succeeded in getting a certain trade union to post a description and photograph of a missing man on its bulletin boards. This aided in finding the man. Fraternal orders may be used in the same way, though for many reasons they cannot be so helpful as the trades unions.

Employment agencies should not be forgotten in seeking to trace a man through his industrial record. The extension of the federal employment service, with free inter-city communication, should be of assistance in getting upon the track of deserters.

The co-operation of newspapers can be secured to good effect in tracing missing men.

Herbert McCann, who had been doing railway construction in Russia, returned to this country and disappeared while en route from an eastern city to his home in Canada. There was reason to think that he might have left the train in an intoxicated condition at an

FINDING THE DESERTING HUSBAND

important junction point; and the family social agency of that city was asked to trace him. No information was secured from the police, lodging houses, employment agencies, etc., and finally the following advertisement was inserted in the local paper: "*Information Wanted*—Anyone knowing the whereabouts of Herbert McCann, Montreal, who returned from Russia in June, will confer a favor upon his family by notifying Social Service Building, 34 Grand Street." Six days later a reply was received from a man in a nearby town, and McCann was found at work in a factory there.

More than upon any other method the National Desertion Bureau depends on the publication of pictures and short newspaper paragraphs. As this Bureau deals entirely with Jewish deserters, it works chiefly through the Yiddish newspapers. Its "Gallery of Missing Husbands" is a regular weekly feature in some of the better known of these journals, and attracts increasingly wide attention. The Bureau estimates that 70 per cent of the deserters which it finds are discovered through the publication of pictures. It should be remembered, however, that this Bureau is dealing with a selected group, who know a great deal about one another, live closely together, follow in the main only a few trades, and read only a limited number of foreign-language newspapers. Whether anything like the same results could be obtained by the same methods applied to deserting husbands of many different national and social backgrounds is open to question.

Since most deserters leave the city, if not the state, the social worker who is dealing with the family problem is often not the same person to whom is delegated the task of finding the man. This fact makes necessary the most careful and sympathetic co-operation between the social workers or agencies, which must work together at long range upon the problem. In the case of Herbert McCann, just cited, not less than four family social work societies were concerned —three in the United States and one in Canada. This necessitated keeping in the closest touch, by letter and telegram, so that each was informed of the doings of the others. Such a piece of work calls for a common body of experience and technique among the workers concerned, amounting almost to an unwritten under-

FINDING THE DESERTING HUSBAND

standing as to how the work should be done. Nothing makes more fascinating reading than the record of a quick, touch-and-go investigation, such as is presented in the finding of a deserter conducted by skilled case workers who are accustomed to work together. Much can, under these circumstances, be taken for granted or left to the discretion of the worker or agency whose help is being sought. There are instances, however, where no such common understanding exists, and where the home-town agency has to work through people with little social training or with training of a type which definitely unfits them properly to approach the deserting man. It is a distressing experience to know that a man has slipped through one's fingers, been frightened off or alienated, by poor work at the other end. Are there any ways to reduce the number of these mischances?

Even with the closest co-operation among case workers of ability in different cities the results are not always as favorable, for obvious reasons, as if the person who knows the family were the one to find and interview the man. More and

BROKEN HOMES

more it is realized that money and time spent in going to nearby cities to do one's own investigating is well spent. There used to be a feeling on the part of the kindred society whose territory was thus invaded that this action argued lack of confidence in its work; but as the importance of the personal contact has been more widely recognized this feeling has disappeared. It may be said that a worker who goes to a strange city is handicapped by her lack of knowledge of local conditions. This is of course true, and it may easily be a question of how great an advantage will be gained by the journey. The worker from the man's home town can, however, go far toward overcoming the handicap of unfamiliarity with the place, as well as toward dispelling any sense of injury in the mind of a professional colleague, by calling first at the office of the local agency and talking the problem over thoroughly, consulting the map and getting what hints the local agency may be able to furnish. The first question to ask oneself, therefore, is "Will it not be worth while to go myself?"

If for geographical or other reasons this is

FINDING THE DESERTING HUSBAND

impracticable, the next thing that should receive careful consideration is the type of letter to be written. If the situation is very emergent (as in the case of Adolph R. cited earlier), the request may have to be sent by telegraph; but even in a telegram it is possible to convey some detail. To try to save money by confining oneself to ten words is unwise. If time admits, a letter is more desirable, and the principle of its construction is as simple as the Golden Rule—give the other person all the information you would like to have if you were receiving the letter. Where the correspondent is not a trained social worker, very specific suggestions and directions should be given as to how you wish the man dealt with if found.

There might also be laid down a Golden Rule for recipients of requests from out-of-town that missing men be traced. "Give the request right-of-way over your regular work, and send back as prompt and as full a reply as you would wish yourself" might adequately cover the case. A reply which contains a history of actual steps taken as well as results gained, is more satis-

BROKEN HOMES

factory than one which does not. Good case workers believe in reciprocity and treat their neighbor's problem as their own. "We heard that a man we were interested in was in the vicinity of a certain city, and in the effort to trace him wrote to the charity organization society in that place, but without success. Several months later the charity organization society saw an item in a newspaper to the effect that the man had been interned as an enemy alien, and notified us. (This shows no cleverness on our part, but good work by the other society.)"

V

FURTHER ITEMS IN THE INVESTIGATION

IT IS evident that the need of finding the man strongly influences the course of this type of investigation, especially in the early stages. Are there other considerations, however, that modify the technique of inquiry into these desertion cases?

There is one crisis in the lives of deserted families which is not duplicated in the history of any other group suffering from social disability. This crisis is the period of the first desertion. "If we could learn what preceded and what immediately followed the first desertion, we should know much more than we do now about how to deal with the problem," said a case worker who has studied many court records.

The *number* of subsequent desertions may be

both interesting and significant, but the circumstances attending them are not nearly so well worth study as are those connected with the critical first break. We should go back to that spot and probe for causes. The common practice of recording carefully what led up to a chronic deserter's last desertion before his family applied, and of passing over his earlier desertions with a mere mention of their number and dates, puts the emphasis in the wrong place.

We must, however, go further back than the first desertion for a working fund of knowledge. The importance of knowing what were the influences surrounding the man and woman in childhood and youth has already been dwelt upon and is so generally conceded as to need no elaboration here. Of especial value also is careful inquiry into the period of courtship, the circumstances of the marriage, and the history of the earlier married life. "We should seek to know what first drew them together, as well as what forced them apart," said a thoughtful district secretary. The notorious unhappiness of "forced marriages" leads case workers to scruti-

FURTHER ITEMS IN THE INVESTIGATION

nize the relation between the date of marriage and the date of the birth of the first child. It should be remembered, however, that not all marriages which are entered into during pregnancy are forced marriages. Studies of forced marriages, so-called, have not always taken this fact into consideration.

The superintendent of a state department for aid to widows made a study of the vital statistics of 500 families chosen at random. She states that "out of these 500 mothers 96, or 19.2 per cent, had conceived out of wedlock—or rather before wedlock—judging by the date of marriage and that of the first child's birth. All these women were hard working; several of good standing in the neighborhood and the mothers of large families of children." This group of homes represents by no means an unstable segment of the community, since in most instances the couples had lived together in reasonable harmony up to the time of the man's death. But do the 96 represent forced marriages as ordinarily thought of by the social worker? The study just quoted has no facts bearing upon

BROKEN HOMES

this point. The likelihood is that a large number of these marriages, termed forced, were in reality not brought about by outside pressure at all, but that the couple were intending to be married at the time the pregnancy occurred and that the circumstances were condoned by public opinion in the community where the marriage took place.

The Chicago Juvenile Protective Association, however, has made a study of 89 forced marriages which were brought about in connection with bastardy proceedings. In this study there is no attempt to differentiate as to the *amount* of unwillingness that had had to be overcome on the part of either the man or the woman. Fifty-three of the women said that the marriage had been entered into willingly on their part. Sixty of them stated that they were well treated by their husbands, and only five complained of abuse or unkindness. Out of the 89 marriages brought about after proceedings were instituted 69 of the couples were still living together from one to two years later, although 20, or nearly

FURTHER ITEMS IN THE INVESTIGATION

one in five, had separated before the two-year period was over.*

A young woman with four small children was given advice by an associated charities about her approaching confinement, and no further inquiry was made at that time. She was living apart from her husband, who was contributing a small amount regularly. The income was inadequate and it was decided to push the matter further. Efforts to verify the marriage failed. Finally, a tactful worker was able to learn that the ceremony had not taken place until after the birth of the first three children, that the couple had had sexual relations since the woman was a girl of fifteen, and that her relatives had never known the true state of affairs. The man's mother finally interfered, and urged her son not to live with his wife. After much careful work, and with the assistance of a co-operating priest, a plan was worked out which brought the couple together and induced them to move away from the region in which the man's parents lived.

A probation department tells of a case where, although the man was unwilling to marry, a court marriage was brought about; the man made his payments promptly and observed the other conditions of his probation faithfully. The woman, however, was indifferent to any efforts to bring about a reconciliation. It was finally discovered

* Bowen, Louise de K.: A Study of Bastardy Cases. Juvenile Protective Association of Chicago, 1914.

BROKEN HOMES

that she was immoral. The case culminated in the securing of a divorce by the man, who was granted the custody of the children.

The same department submits a story where good results were obtained in subsequently reconciling, after a desertion, a couple whose marriage had been of the forced description. The probation department arranged for the couple to live apart in the early stage of probationary treatment. A careful study was made of each of the individuals, and in their sincere attachment a basis was discovered for re-establishment of the home under the supervision of the probation officer. Five years later the man was found to be at work at the same position originally obtained for him by the probation officer, his salary had been increased, the family had grown in number and were getting on extremely well.

Although the term "forced marriage" has come to have the meaning given above, unions can be really forced where there has been no sex relation before marriage. In one unhappy marriage which came finally to a court of domestic relations, the wife was a weak and timid woman who married her husband because of her fear that he would carry out his threat and kill her and himself if she refused him. Another, an Italian girl, was married at fourteen by her parents against her inclinations to a well-to-do

FURTHER ITEMS IN THE INVESTIGATION

man, much older than she, who was a lodger in the family. As she grew to womanhood their incompatibility increased; finally, after four children had been born, the family was broken up and the children committed to institutions.

There are compulsions and false motives, operating to bring about marriages, which spring from within not without; and the discovery of any motive for the marriage except mutual inclination has significance to the case worker. Light was thrown on the troubles of one young couple when the girl confessed that she had married a youth for whom she had no particular affection, in order to "spite" her relatives and assert her right to do as she chose. And the unfortunate young woman who married a street evangelist in a fit of religious enthusiasm, and because of his promise that they would travel about the world saving souls together, had a married life both short and stormy. The so-called "slacker marriages" of the few months preceding the first draft in 1917 illustrate this point. The wreckage of these marriages is

BROKEN HOMES

already drifting in increasing amount to the courts of domestic relations.

One of the most important items in desertion cases, and one far too often neglected, is the verification of the marriage. Much seeming indifference and confusion on this point is probably caused by the quasi-legality in many states of common law marriages. The case worker should not forget, however, that a common law union is often only a device on the part of one or the other of the two to avoid prosecution for bigamy. When it is established that the marriage is a common law union, a strong suspicion should be set up in the worker's mind that there may be some legal barrier to a ceremony, and careful inquiry should be directed along this line. Not only does the verification of a marriage give the worker a sound basis on which to proceed to court action if necessary, but the copy of the actual marriage record, where that can be procured, gives much valuable information as to dates, addresses, and names of relatives and witnesses. A transcript of the record will usually be furnished by the registrar of vital statistics

FURTHER ITEMS IN THE INVESTIGATION

in the city where the marriage took place (if in the United States) for a nominal fee of fifty cents.

It is much more difficult to verify marriages which took place in other countries, and social workers are often appalled by the prevalence of the so-called "American marriage" among immigrant deserters, who trust to our happy-go-lucky methods for protection against a prosecution for bigamy.

Such was the case of Orfeo Pelligrini, who came to this country and took a new wife when his children in Italy were nearly grown. His Italian family came to America through their own efforts a few years later, and Orfeo found that he had underestimated the character of his eldest son, who traced his father, had him arrested and taken to the city where his original family was living. Orfeo, now forcibly reunited to the wife of his bosom, walks softly under the threat of bigamy proceedings, while the "American" wife refuses to take any action on the ground that "he didn't go away from me of his own wish, and why should I put him behind the bars?"

Of an altogether more simple mental make-up was the Slovak laborer who brought his pregnant "American wife" and two children to the district office of a charity organization society, saying that the relatives in Europe of Anna, his first wife, had sent Anna to this country, and she was on the point of arriving. He added that, as manifestly it was not possible to support two families on his wages, he would like to provide for his second wife through "the Charity."

A district secretary who has worked for many years with Italians is authority for the statement that marriages in Italy are always registered at the man's legal residence, no matter where the marriage took place. "Careful Italian parents, if they cannot get reliable information in other ways, write to the 'paese' of a suitor for information in regard to his conjugal condition. A marriage which takes place in America is customarily registered with the consul for transmission to the home town in Italy."

In some countries of Latin America great confusion may be caused by the fact that a marriage performed in church is not legal in the eyes of the state unless a second ceremony is gone through before the civil authorities. A Guatemalan woman, deserted in this country, had no recourse in law because she had had only the church ceremony in her country. Her claim to

FURTHER ITEMS IN THE INVESTIGATION

the status of common law wife was invalidated by the man's producing proof that he was already married at the time the religious ceremony was performed.

Having established the fact that a legal marriage has taken place, the case worker must keep in mind the possibility that it may have been later dissolved. It is not at all uncommon to find that a deserter who has gone off with another woman has started proceedings to get a divorce by "publication." This can happen when the two have gone to a state where such unfair divorce procedure is permitted. Publication in these cases takes place in local newspapers which there is little or no chance of the wife seeing; and she may later find herself a divorced woman with no legal claim for support for herself or children, and suffering under charges of misconduct without having had a chance of being heard. The National Desertion Bureau found this proceeding so common an abuse that it established a clearing bureau in its central office, and its local representatives in different parts of the country notify this bureau

BROKEN HOMES

as soon as any action for divorce is started by a man with a Jewish name against a wife whose "address is unknown."*

What are some of the other points at which the investigation of cases of desertion may differ from the technique generally accepted? The superintendent of a desertion bureau, in answer to this question, said that he emphasized "neighborhood references" more than in the ordinary case. Social workers have become very wary, of course, of much inquiry among present neighbors; but where the protection of the woman or the children is involved it is often necessary to procure the testimony of people who live nearby or in the same house. A deserted family is usually so much a center of neighborhood interest or sympathy, or both, that it is easier than in some other types of cases to secure information from neighbors, tradesmen, and so on, without augmenting neighborhood gossip.

* It is the policy of the Bureau, when such a case is discovered, to help the wife get competent legal advice in the city where action is being brought, and either to contest the case or start a counter suit. Where necessary the woman is sent on to appear in person.

FURTHER ITEMS IN THE INVESTIGATION

Probably the most difficult part of the necessary information to be secured in desertion cases is an adequate picture of the sex relationship between man and wife. The part which sex plays in the causation of desertion has been touched upon in Chapter II.* In getting the information from the people concerned, the case worker needs no elaborate equipment as a psycho-analyst; but she should know enough about sex psychology to recognize a pathological problem when she meets it, and to be able to call on the psycho-analyst or psychiatrist for specialized service.

The securing of an adequate picture of the sex life of the couple may have to be delegated, however, to some volunteer whose own sex, profession, or marital experience makes him or her a suitable person to secure it.

"The majority of social case workers are unmarried women under forty, and in this particular respect they frequently find themselves handicapped by the natural reluctance of the deserter to discuss his conceptions of the marital relation in such a way as to be enlightening to them, as well as by the chivalrous attitude which the

* See p. 37 sq.

BROKEN HOMES

woman of the tenements often adopts toward her unmarried visitor. The decisive statement, 'You have never been married, so you can't understand,' often proves at least a temporary barrier in dealing with deserted wives, just as the similar statement, 'You have never been a mother so you cannot know the feelings of one,' is used to block her efforts in another direction. If it is found impossible to carry on the necessary discussions rationally and without too serious embarrassment, it is often possible to call upon the socially-minded physician or clergyman for help along this line."*

To sum up, the interviews with the family and the supplementary visits and letters of inquiry should furnish the social worker if possible with:

1. A clear picture of the home in which the two adult members of the family grew up, and the factors in their early training which contributed to their failure as husband or wife; or which can be utilized as assets in the future plan.

2. A history of how the couple met; the events of their courtship and marriage, including

* J. C. Colcord n *The Annals of the American Academy of Political and Social Science*, May, 1918, p. 97.

FURTHER ITEMS IN THE INVESTIGATION

sex relations prior to marriage with spouse or others; also previous marriages. Records of marriage, death of previous spouse, etc., are very important and should be secured if in existence.

3. A picture of the family and its individual members in their other social relationships—with employers, medical agencies, teachers, their church, their friends, their relatives. Knowledge of their habits, tastes, and characteristics, with special attention to period of first desertion. Analysis of factors leading to the desertion.

4. History of first reconciliation (unless the present is the first break). History of subsequent desertions. Court record, if any.

A prerequisite to some of the above information is an interview or interviews with the man. Where this cannot be had as part of the first investigation, the investigation should leave the worker in possession of some good clues, at least, to the man's whereabouts.

VI

THE DETAILS OF TREATMENT

AS IN all other problems faced by the case worker, it is impossible to lay down general rules for the treatment of desertion. There may be general considerations, however, which it is well to keep in mind, some of which have been advanced in the last chapter.*

On questions of investigation there is closer agreement among social workers than on questions of treatment. Personal factors here play a much larger part, and it may very well be that two case workers who differ in personality but are of equal ability, will choose very different plans of treatment in a given case and yet each bring it to a successful issue. It is with a good

* The Questionnaire on the Deserted Family (see p. 395 sq. of Richmond's Social Diagnosis) has already been mentioned as suggesting lines of investigation. It will also be found useful at the stage of summing up knowledge gained and seeing in what direction it points.

THE DETAILS OF TREATMENT

deal of hesitancy, therefore, that a case worker ventures upon the discussion of anything so flexible as treatment. In preparation for this study many consultations were had with practising social case workers in the fields of family work, probation, medical-social service, and child welfare. Differences of opinion were found and this chapter will attempt to express the composite opinion on how to treat the deserter and his family in the different situations which confront them.

1. Man's Whereabouts Unknown but Desertion of Recent Date.—It is better in this case to make no very definite plans for the family. Emergent plans, both as to relief and medical or other care should, of course, be prompt and adequate. Now is the time, if it can be done, to win the confidence and co-operation of the wife. We should, however, make no promises for the sake of "buying" co-operation, and give no premature advice either as to prosecution or reconciliation. Everything possible should be done to strengthen such ties with church, relatives, and friends as

BROKEN HOMES

may be helpful, but the social worker should be slow to encourage the family to form new ties with other social agencies at this time. She should avoid the possibility of judging the woman harshly in a period of stress, but be watchful for signs of deterioration and resourceful to combat them. This is the stage, of course, when all energies should be bent toward finding the man.

In this as in the other situations about to be discussed, the question of whether or not the home should be broken up and the children committed should be decided on other grounds than on the desertion alone. Under many circumstances, it is the best thing to do. The woman, worn out with anxiety or abuse, may be unequal to their physical care for the present; or they may be running wild and in danger of becoming delinquent. The mother may be morally an unfit guardian, and the desertion may furnish the long-sought opportunity to interfere for the children's protection. Commitment may have to be planned, and the mother's consent won, to save the children from

THE DETAILS OF TREATMENT

the return of a brutal father, against whom she cannot protect them. Or she may desire a temporary commitment in order to give her husband a severe lesson. The main consideration, however, ought to be what is going, in the long run, to be best for the children concerned.

2. Man's Whereabouts Unknown, Desertion of Long Standing.—A very different problem from the preceding may be presented in the family of a man who disappeared some time ago. Where the desertion is bona fide and has persisted over a period of years, it is often possible to treat the family as if the man were dead, and, if other circumstances make this advisable, to plan comprehensively for the future. There is always the chance, however, that, until the man's death is established, he may turn up unexpectedly. If living, he usually manages to hear now and again about his family and is often able to find them at will. A man who had neither seen nor communicated with his family during the ten years they had been maintained by a private

BROKEN HOMES

family agency, nevertheless sent promptly for his wife and eldest son by a messenger who knew exactly where to find them (although they had moved in the interval several times), when he lay dying of alcoholic excess in the city hospital.

The laws of many states contain a provision that the marriage of a person who has completely disappeared and not been heard from in a period of years can be set aside by the proper authorities. This makes legal the remarriage of the spouse. In nearly all of the states divorce can be obtained on the ground of long continued desertion.* The wisdom of advising such a divorce, however, should receive careful individual consideration, particularly in relation to the religious faith of the client and the attitude of that faith toward divorce.

3. Man's Whereabouts Known; Man Unwilling to Return or Support.—Many types of deserting men are included under this catch-all heading—the

* The state of New York is an exception, as it grants only limited divorce for desertion.

THE DETAILS OF TREATMENT

so-called "justifiable deserter;" the man who has fled to escape his creditors or is a fugitive from justice; the man who has elected to try life with another mate; the wandering hobo who means to come back some sweet day but not now; the cowardly pregnancy deserter; the low grade irresponsible—a motley crew. They are grouped together here for convenience, since they constitute those with whom coercive measures have most often to be used.

A good example of the "justifiable deserter" is found in the story of Williams.* This man, when home conditions became intolerable, tried to secure his children's safety through the courts but did not obtain a hearing. He left home feeling that he was fully justified. The lame point in his self-defense was his failure to support his children, and it took a court order to rectify this in part.

Joseph Mellor is in a more logical situation in his refusal to provide for his wife, since he is paying the board of his child in a good institution. He makes no charge against her character, but insists that her quarrelsome and dictatorial disposition makes her impossible to live with. She had haled him so many times into

* See p. 57.

BROKEN HOMES

court and lost him so many positions that Mellor, who earns a good salary, will deal with her only through his lawyer, who keeps his client's whereabouts secret and will not trust the social worker interested even to the extent of arranging an interview.

It is generally impossible in cases of such deep-seated antagonism to make any plans looking toward reconciliation. The "justifiable deserter" can usually be reasoned with, and once he understands and admits his responsibilities, can often be made to live up to them without judicial process.

A ship steward deserted his wife, who was both alcoholic and paretic, taking with him his only child whom he placed with his relatives. The woman was devoted to the boy and broken in spirit because she was not allowed to see him. The steward claimed, probably correctly, that he was not responsible for the woman's syphilitic condition. The following extract from the record of the first interview with the man is quoted to show the lines of argument which were effective with him:

"Man at District Office—Visitor started in immediately with the subject in hand, thinking he was the sort that would respond to absolutely direct dealing. Explained to him that we had been given to understand his wife was ill, not only from alcoholism but also

THE DETAILS OF TREATMENT

from other complications; that it was suspected there might be some difficulty with her blood and that we had been advised that her mental condition was not now as strong as it had been previously. Explained to him that he was absolutely responsible for his wife, for her support, and for her care and protection, and that no matter how far he traveled, his responsibility remained the same; that he had assumed this when he married her. Said that he felt no responsibility for her whatsoever, that he had done all he ever would do for her and intended to devote his efforts toward his child. Visitor explained to him that woman's intemperance might perfectly well be a disease over which it would be very difficult for her to have control; that, moreover, if she were suffering also from a blood condition, this should have treatment. Explained that he would more nearly meet his responsibilities were he to have her examined and send her where she could procure the treatment required, even if it meant commitment to an institution. At this point man seemed more interested, particularly as visitor told him that Arthur would grow up and would want to know where his mother was and what had become of her; and if man had left her sick and alone, at the mercy of strangers, he would not be able to give an adequate accounting to his son. Man's reaction was not what visitor had expected—he would be glad to put her away where she could not trouble him any more but he did not intend to expend any more money. Said he was under too heavy expenses with Arthur. Claimed he was making $70 a month, and visitor forced him to add

BROKEN HOMES

that he got in addition his board and lodging on the ship, so that he was under no expense except when on shore leave. Visitor repeated that as a husband he was required to pay for woman's care, that that was the right thing to do; that one way he would be a husband deserting his wife, liable to arrest for non-support and desertion, and the other way a husband with a sick wife for whom he was willing to provide the medical attention and care that every sick person has a right to have. He said if it was a question of a few dollars a week, he supposed he would be willing to do it, and visitor felt he really was willing to do the right thing if he only could be assured that woman would not interfere with Arthur. Said he would never let woman see the child, but finally admitted, if she were not drunk and was in the hospital and it would do any good, he supposed she could."

With persistent or recalcitrant deserters as a group, court action has very often to be invoked. Procedure in this direction differs so much in different communities that only general observations can be offered here. If the man has left his home but not the town and is still within the jurisdiction of the local court, the magistrate will usually issue a summons (which in many cities the wife is expected to serve) calling on the man to appear at court on the

THE DETAILS OF TREATMENT

date set for the hearing. If he fails to appear a warrant for his arrest is issued. If he has left the city but not the state, local courts may issue warrants, which can be mailed to the city to which the man has gone and served by the police there; or an officer may be sent from the home town with a warrant to arrest the man and bring him back.

Prior to his arraignment, the best court practice calls for an investigation by the probation officer, so that the judge may have substantiated facts before him when the case comes up. Whether this is done or not here is the time and place for the social worker who already knows the family to get his knowledge in usable fashion before the court. How best to do this varies greatly in different communities. Sometimes the social worker is permitted to talk the matter over with the judge personally, sometimes with the probation officer, clerk or other court official. Sometimes a written report is required, to be attached to the probation officer's report. Occasionally the social worker gets no chance to be heard unless he is present

BROKEN HOMES

to testify in open court. In the last two contingencies, care must be taken to safeguard information given in confidence, even by the deserter. Letters marked "confidential" should not ordinarily be submitted in court except by consent of the writer, as some judges hold that material so submitted becomes a matter of public record.

The approach to the court, therefore, is governed by local conditions. A very important part of co-operation in any community is to see that this channel is kept free from obstruction. In general, the probation officer should be the best friend of the other social workers, since he knows their language. Indeed, many social workers themselves combine the office of probation officer with their other duties.

After the institution of court proceedings the outside social worker has usually little chance to affect the disposition of the case. This is made by the judge on the basis of the testimony he elicits in court, and on that of any preliminary investigation he may have caused to be made. Disposition may be:

THE DETAILS OF TREATMENT

1. In rare instances, to dismiss the complaint altogether.

2. To remand for a later hearing.

3. To induce the woman to drop her complaint and give the man another chance.*

4. To place the man under court order to stay away from home and pay his wife a stated amount weekly. Custom differs in different places as to whether payment shall be direct to the wife, through the probation officer or clerk of court, or through public or private charities.

5. To order the man to return home and contribute a stated amount.

6. To place on probation (together with either 4 or 5).

7. Commitment—usually to jail or workhouse, and for a period of not over six months. May be longer for violation of probation or for aggravated offense.

When the deserting man has gone without the borders of the state, there is the added problem of securing his extradition, which is often a difficult one. Wife desertion is in most states only a misdemeanor (in New York it is even less serious and constitutes in the eye of the law only disorderly conduct). Since extradition between states has to be acted upon by the governors of the states, it is unusual (though

---

* See p. 132 sq. concerning court reconciliations.

BROKEN HOMES

not impossible*) to secure extradition for a misdemeanor. The reluctance of the authorities is understandable, however, when it is realized that to extradite for wife desertion would be to create a precedent for extradition for any sort of misdemeanor. There is in most states a law which makes the abandonment of a minor child or children a felony, punishable by a long term in state prison, and it is this law which is generally invoked when the man has been traced to another state. Complaint then has to be made to the district (or county) attorney, the matter taken before the grand jury and an indictment secured before extradition papers can be granted. The man, if captured, must usually be tried in a higher court than the domestic relations court; if convicted he is likely to be more severely punished. Extradition means expense to the state; it is usually difficult, moreover, to get an active interest taken in

---

* See Baldwin, Wm. H.: "The Most Effective Methods of Dealing with Cases of Desertion and Non-support," *Journal American Institute of Criminal Law and Criminology*, November, 1917.

THE DETAILS OF TREATMENT

extraditing a family deserter who, to the legal eye, has committed an offense neither against the person nor against property, and cannot therefore be a serious offender!

If extradition for family desertion is difficult between states, with other countries it is impossible, as no treaties exist even with contiguous countries like Canada and Mexico.* By special arrangement with the Canadian authorities, states which touch the Canadian border can sometimes obtain the person of a deserter without actual extradition. Information is submitted to the police of the Canadian town where the man is known to be, who thereupon arrest him as an "undesirable citizen" and arrange for his deportation. The neighboring state is notified, and an officer with a warrant meets the Canadian officer and the prisoner at the boundary, arresting the latter as soon as he sets foot across the state line.

The testimony of social workers is, in the main, in favor of probation as against long prison sentence for men of this type. "We have found a

* See p. 169 sq.

shortened penitentiary sentence, with release on probation, very successful in a number of instances." "Sometimes the probation has been more effective by its being a sort of double probation; that is, having the case pending in juvenile court as well as municipal or district court. The fear of having his children permanently taken from him if he again fails to support them has, in one or two instances, had much more effect with the deserter than the threat of a prison sentence." "Probation works very well and occasionally a prison sentence; but probation is better." These statements come from cities where probation work is well organized. From another city where the probation officers are notoriously overworked, comes a pessimistic note: "The theory of probation is fine, but the practice is poor because the officers have entirely too much to do."

Probation is simply case work with the added "punch" of the law behind it; so that when it is at all well done it should have the more lasting results. Probation officers and other social workers agree, however, that for certain deserters

THE DETAILS OF TREATMENT

of the complacent type, an unexpected prison sentence is sometimes a very salutary dash of cold water.

After having tried one or two short absences, ostensibly to look for work and finding that nothing serious happened to him, Andreas Gorokhoff walked out one day and did not come back for five years. During that time his wife's relatives and the community's family agency took care of his family while he led the life of a care-free vagabond. He was ready upon his return to settle down again for a time; but the family agency and the probation department thought differently, and succeeded in having him sent to state prison for an indeterminate sentence of not more than two years. He was released on parole for good conduct, returned home, went to work, and, during the four years which have since elapsed, all has gone well.

Good results may, and probably more often do, follow shorter prison sentences.

A man on probation for intemperance, broke it and deserted. On account of the children's keen feeling about the consequent disgrace, the wife made no move until urged thereto by the social worker interested. Her husband was then arrested in a nearby city and brought back, much surprised at the firm stand his wife had taken. He was sentenced to four months, served two, and was released on parole. Since his return he has not been drinking and has been contributing satisfactorily toward the support of his family.

The first step taken by Harvey Brand when released from the workhouse after a short prison sentence, was to stop in at a furniture store and order a green plush parlor "suit" on the instalment plan. Harvey had never been conspicuously interested in his home before, and the district secretary and her committee were aghast at this new evidence of his irresponsibility. The green plush was, however, the outward sign of an inner burgeoning, and it warmed the heart of Mrs. Harvey as nothing else could have done. From that time, Harvey, with judicious encouragement over a few hard spots, has become a good family man and a regular provider.

The particular problem involved in the treatment of the family during the trial and imprisonment of the deserter is that of encouraging the woman to stick to her guns. If she withdraws her complaint or secures his release before his time is up, she not only convinces him of her lack of firmness but the entry in the court record seriously prejudices her case should she make complaint there again. Unless the social worker is convinced, therefore, that the sentence has been unduly severe, the wife should be encouraged in every way to let her husband serve

THE DETAILS OF TREATMENT

out his time. If a policy of relief has been necessary, care should be taken that it be adequate, so that economic pressure will not induce her to ask for his release. If the home has been broken up and the children committed, the mother's loneliness and desire to have her home back is likely to work in the same way. The hope of making her husband kinder when he returns often leads a woman to ask for his release. The pressure of relatives and friends, and sometimes of her church is likely to be exerted in the same direction and unknown to the social worker. Chaplains of correctional institutions, interested entirely in the man and with no knowledge of the family situation, are also likely to appear in the case; and it is well to acquaint them, in the beginning, of our interest and our hope that no step will be taken without a consultation. If it is hoped or expected that the man will return to his home after imprisonment, he should be earnestly cultivated by the social worker while he is serving his time. Visits and letters will go far toward breaking down his resentment at the part the

BROKEN HOMES

worker is likely to have played in "putting him behind the bars." Now is an excellent time to introduce a man as volunteer visitor to the prisoner, if he is to be off probation when released. If imprisonment or "stay-away probation" does not have the desired effect of making the deserter willing and anxious to return to his family and take care of them, or if for any reason return is permanently undesirable, the advisability of obtaining a legal separation* should be considered at this point. If, on the other hand, the man evinces eagerness to return home and support his family, he comes automatically (though belatedly) into the class to be considered in the next chapter.

* See p. 127.

VII

THE DETAILS OF TREATMENT (Continued)

THERE remains a fourth classification under treatment, of cases which demand even more individualized care and therefore more extended comment than those just considered.

4. Man's Whereabouts Known; Man Willing to Return.—Here the question to determine is whether it is going to be a desirable thing for the man to re-enter the home and, if so, when. This does not always lie within the power of the case worker to decide; the couple may and often do resolve their differences for the time being without reference to her opinion. But she can often hasten, defer, or even prevent the reconciliation. Careful consideration must be given the elements involved: What causes probably operated to bring about the rupture in family relations? If there have been other desertions what does their history show? Is the man's willingness to return a sign of real change of heart and purpose, or is he merely afraid of punishment? Are his habits such as to make him a fit inmate of the home? Is he capable of supporting the family? Can any adjustment of temperaments be made which will lessen incompatibility? Is the wife willing to have him return? What are her motives? Has she enough firmness of character to carry out a plan to which she has agreed? These are only a few of the questions to which the social worker needs to know the answer, if the decision is to be a wise one.

If none of the elements is present in the home out of which family life can be reconstructed, if the man's self-indulgence and cruelty have been proved beyond any doubt, or if affection is dead or never existed, then the decision may have to be that no reconciliation be attempted. In many cases the question then is how best to protect the woman and children against the man's forcing his way upon them. Court intervention is usually necessary here, if it has not

THE DETAILS OF TREATMENT

already taken place; and a first step is to have the husband placed under a court order to give separate support and to stay away from his home.* The wife should be armed with a warrant for his arrest, which can be served by the policeman on the beat if the man appears. Such a man usually considers that his proprietorship of the home and the family is not affected by his absence or even by court orders, and when fortified by liquor he is likely to force his entrance into the home and perhaps do harm. The protection of the warrant is not absolute; in such cases as this it ought later to be reinforced by a legal separation. Social workers avail themselves of this resource far less than they should. It controverts the principles of no religious sect and gives all the protection of absolute divorce (including the payment of alimony) to the woman and children. To the children it is likely to give more protection than divorce; for in the event of the divorced husband's remarriage the children of the second wife have prior rights over those of the first, and legal separation makes this

* See p. 179 regarding equity powers of the courts.

BROKEN HOMES

impossible by preventing the remarriage of either party. Proceedings for a legal separation cannot usually be started if a man is on probation, but may be while he is undergoing imprisonment. It should be said that, after a separation, claims for non-payment of alimony cannot, in many states, be pressed in a court of domestic relations but must go to a civil court. This is usually more expensive and less satisfactory.*

Some social workers even advance the heretical doctrine that support secured through the court from a cruel and dangerous husband does not make up for the harm he may do and the anxiety he causes. If to force him into periodical payments means that he will be continually excited into seeking out and "beating up" his offending wife, the support she is able to extort from him comes high. It is sometimes necessary to move a family to new quarters and actually help them to hide from the pursuit of one of these insistent

---

* Massachusetts social workers succeeded in 1917 in securing the passage of a law which permits the ordinary non-support law to be invoked in case of the man's failure to pay the amount ordered after a legal separation.

THE DETAILS OF TREATMENT

gentry. Even if we have some doubt that the wife's protestations of fear or aversion are genuine, we should hardly take the risk of revealing her address if she wishes it kept secret. This precaution applies not only to the man but to anyone whom we suspect of being interested on his behalf. A district secretary continued to refuse the address of his family to a dangerous epileptic deserter who threatened the secretary's life and, in the opinion of physicians who examined him, was likely to carry out his threat.

The committee on difficult cases in a family social agency voted to refuse to accept voluntary payments from a thoroughly worthless deserter and transmit them to his wife whose address he was seeking to learn, on the theory that it was better for her and her children to be entirely quit of him, and that nothing would make him realize the finality of the decision more than to refuse his money. The agency, it was felt, would be in better position to protect the wife and children if it refused to act as post office for the man.

The same consideration might apply in questions of extradition. When the whereabouts of a deserter of this type has been discovered in another city a safe distance away, it may be

BROKEN HOMES

wiser to sacrifice the money he might be forced to contribute than to have him brought within arm's length of his wife and family.

A prime difficulty in dealing with the undesirable husband who is willing to come home is often the attitude of the wife. Some of the causes at work when a woman takes her husband back have been discussed earlier.* Unfortunately, hopelessly bad husbands profit by them as well as hopeful ones. The policy of niggardly relief to a deserted wife has undoubtedly been responsible for many of these unfortunate attempts to patch up a life together. "She was worn down by her efforts to keep the household going, and, when the faint chance of her husband's supporting her appeared, she took it" is the explanation given by a case worker of one unpromising reconciliation, and she goes on to say of this and another similar story: "With both of these it seems that enough money put into the household to enable these mothers to be with their children more and to keep up a reasonable standard of health for themselves

* See p. 13 sq.

THE DETAILS OF TREATMENT

might have resulted in their refusing to take back their husbands. . . . Our records seem to show that inadequate relief, making life fairly hard for the deserted mother, does not tend to keep the man from returning or others from deserting."

The story of Mrs. Francis shows the effect of adequate relief in strengthening her decision not to take her husband back. He had been a chronic deserter for years, had drank heavily, been foul mouthed and abusive, while failing to support the family when at home, so that Mrs. Francis had only a little harder time when he was away. His last desertion took place when she was near confinement. Owing to her condition, the church and a family agency co-operated in an unusually generous relief policy. This was in a state which gave mother's aid to deserted wives. After about a year this was secured for her, and the health of woman and children was built up and the home improved. Then Mr. Francis sent ambassadors in the form of relatives, with whom Mrs. Francis refused to treat. He later appeared himself, but she would not consider taking him back. He escaped before he could be brought into court. As he has now been gone over two years, it seems that her stand is a genuine one.

On the other hand, when the man has been found and interviewed, he may show signs of repentance, and the earlier history, together with the opinion which the social worker has been able to form about the character of man and woman may make it seem that a reconciliation should be encouraged. A further question then arises: Shall the man return to his home at once or first undergo a probationary period?

The quick reconciliation has been a feature of the work in domestic relations courts from the beginning of the movement. In connection with some courts there are special officers whose duty it is to prevail upon couples who come to the court to patch up their differences and give each other another trial. This would be an admirable procedure if the couples to receive such treatment were selected by a process of careful investigation, and if probationary supervision were continued long enough to ascertain whether permanent results could be secured. As it actually works out it is a little like expecting a wound to heal "by first intention" when it has not been cleaned out thoroughly, and when no attention is being paid to subsequent dressings.

THE DETAILS OF TREATMENT

"The wholesale attempt to patch the tattered fabric of family life in a series of hurried interviews held in the court room, and without any information about the problem except what can be gained from the two people concerned, can hardly be of permanent value in most cases. It is natural that case workers, keenly aware as they are of the slow and difficult processes involved in character-rebuilding, look askance at the court-made reconciliations. With the best will in the world, the people who attempt this delicate service very often have neither the time nor the facts about the particular case in question to give the skilful and devoted personal service necessary to reconstruction. As a result many weak-willed wrong-doers are encouraged to take a pledge of good conduct which they will not, or cannot, keep; and other individuals who feel themselves deeply wronged go away with an additional sense of those wrongs having been underestimated and of having received no redress. The results are written in discouragement and in repeated failures to live in harmony, each of which makes a permanent solution more and more difficult. The case worker to whom the results of the externally imposed reconciliation come back again and again has reason to be confirmed in a distrust of short-cut methods."*

A probation officer writes: "Superficial reconciliations invariably result unsatisfactorily. In one case a recon-

* Colcord, J. C.: Article on "Desertion and Non-support." *Annals of the American Academy of Political and Social Science*, May, 1918, p. 95.

BROKEN HOMES

ciliation was effected before the husband was released on probation. This was done apparently in the hope that it would influence the court in the disposition of the case. After a study of the situation had been made by the probation officer, it was found that the wife was totally incompetent as a housekeeper, that she possessed an antagonistic disposition, had a violent temper, and that no sincere attachment for each other existed between the couple. Before any constructive measures could be carried out by the probation officer to remedy this situation they separated, and it was not possible thereafter to adjust the differences with any degree of satisfaction.

"On another occasion a man who had a previous prison record and had displayed criminal tendencies was arrested for desertion. His wife, a feeble-minded woman with one child, was being maintained at a private institution at county expense. Through the efforts of the district attorney a reconciliation was effected before the case was disposed of in court, and the man was placed on probation upon the recommendation of the prosecutor without the usual preliminary investigation by the probation department. The couple began to live together contrary to the advice of the probation officer. About two months later the man was arrested for committing a series of burglaries and the woman was found to be pregnant. Efforts which had been made by the probation department to determine her mentality disclosed her to be feeble-minded; later she was committed to a custodial institution for feeble-minded women of child-bearing age. The man was committed to a state prison."

THE DETAILS OF TREATMENT

However, when youth and high temper seem to have caused the trouble and there is real affection to build upon, a speedy resumption of life together is usually the best thing.

A young woman with one baby said that her husband had got drunk and threatened her with a knife. They quarreled and he went to relatives in another city. Neighbors testified how devoted the couple had been to each other, describing the young man as handy about the house though "lazy about finding work." He was visited by the family social agency in the city to which he had gone, and wrote a penitent letter asking to come home. The wife agreed; the man immediately returned, got work, and succeeded in overcoming his incipient bad habits. The death of the baby soon after his return seemed only to draw the couple more closely together. The case was soon after closed; nothing has been heard in the three years since to indicate that any further trouble has developed.

A study recently made under the auspices of the Philadelphia Court of Domestic Relations seems to show somewhat better results from court reconciliations than might have been expected. One thousand and two couples who were reconciled in court during the year 1916 were visited from six to eighteen months later.

BROKEN HOMES

Three hundred and ten had separated or had had further differences which brought them to court; 87 could not be found, and 605, or about 60 per cent, were found to be still living together, though with a varying degree of marital happiness, as the report somewhat drily states.*

It should be said that many of these families were probably under the supervision of a probation officer for a longer or shorter period after the reconciliation took place. There is no statement as to the number of repeated deserters among the men, and we cannot estimate how many of the 605 fell within the group which might chance to have the proper basis for reconciliation.

The practice of the Desertion Bureau maintained by the New York Association for Improving the Condition of the Poor is as a rule not to advise reconciliations without a definite preliminary period during which the man shall contribute regularly and show that he means business. "The kind of reconciliation that lasts is the one that is effected with some difficulty

* Philadelphia Municipal Court, Report for 1916, p. 64.

THE DETAILS OF TREATMENT

to the man," its secretary remarked. The same probation department which furnished the stories of hasty and unsuccessful reconciliations,* contributes this remarkable account of the restoration of a family through slow and careful character rebuilding:

George Latham had shamefully neglected his wife and children for several years. He drank to excess, gambled considerably, and associated with women of loose character. He came from good stock, however, and his early training had been excellent. The differences between man and wife seemed impossible to adjust. After the man's release on probation, the co-operation of relatives was secured and through the aid of his new found employer efforts were made toward a reconciliation. The man was gradually led away from his old harmful pursuits and tendencies, these being replaced by wholesome activities. He was induced to join a fraternal organization, to take out insurance for his wife and child, was encouraged to attend church regularly, and to open a bank account. When his sincerity was appreciated by the wife, she agreed to resume housekeeping. Under the direction of the probation officer, new furniture was purchased and the home re-established. This man today holds a responsible position under the employer who aided in his rehabilitation, and occupies a respected place in the community.

*See p. 133.

BROKEN HOMES

Very many processes are indicated in such a story. To bring about the conviction of wrongdoing, to awaken desire and supply an incentive, to keep the hope of attainment alive, to encourage weakened nerves in a new and persistent effort, and all the while to build and strengthen and develop faculties and powers that had been dormant and well-nigh destroyed, is a task that demands a high order of skill and resourcefulness.

The story just told emphasizes the work which was done with the husband. Equally careful work had undoubtedly to be done with the wife to carry her along with the plan. The period of "stay-away probation" for the man is a difficult time for the woman. Neighbors and friends know that he is taking steps in the direction of reformation, and often hold the attitude that it is her duty to let bygones be bygones and receive him again. The promptings of her own heart are often in the same direction; and affection not outlived combines with custom, religious precept, and economic pressure to make it almost impossible to hold to her decision. The

THE DETAILS OF TREATMENT

social worker can sometimes slip some of the burden of the decision off the woman's shoulders to her own by exacting a promise from the two that they will not try living together until the man has "shown what he can do" for a certain definite time. The economic pressure can be eased by a wise policy of relief; but most of all such a woman needs continued encouragement from a person whose judgment and kindliness she has learned to trust. This is another good point at which to introduce the right kind of volunteer visitor, one who will already have established friendly relations with both when the time of readjustment comes, and who can help bridge over that difficult period. In some cases it might be possible and desirable to procure as volunteer visitors to a couple whose marital relations have come to shipwreck, another married couple who have learned how to live together successfully.

The use of carefully chosen volunteers in effecting reconciliations by the case work method has been singularly little developed. In this respect modern theory and practice have both

BROKEN HOMES

fallen behind.* Especially is it an opportunity to enlist the service of men, whom it is easy to interest in a problem that seems to focus about the man of the family. A man volunteer can search for a deserter in places where a woman, by being conspicuous, would defeat her own end. "Located man by mingling with longshoremen on the docks where he usually worked" could hardly be the entry of a woman visitor. A man can also be very useful in court cases, to counteract the prejudice that sometimes exists in court rooms against the testimony of social workers who are women. In the more subtle processes of winning the man's confidence and helping him to regenerate his life and recover his home there is no preponderance of testimony in favor of the man visitor. Sex lines vanish here; the good case worker, man or woman, volunteer or professional, is the person needed.

Sometimes the difficulty is not to deter the

* Miss Richmond, writing in 1895, says: "We would rather have a hundred visitors, patient, intelligent and resourceful, to deal with the married vagabonds of our city, than the best law ever framed, if, in order to get such a law, we must lose the visitors."

THE DETAILS OF TREATMENT

wife from prematurely taking her husband back but to induce her to relent when the proper time comes.

Martin Long was intemperate, his wife was high-tempered; her relatives advised her to leave him and he deserted, leaving the relatives to provide for her and the three children. He was away two years; then, becoming homesick and wanting to re-establish his home if possible, he returned. The wife caused his arrest when he was seeking an interview with her. The probation officer in whose care he was released became convinced of his genuine sincerity and regret, but the wife, still on the advice of her relatives, refused to see him. He persisted in his hope of a reconciliation and made extraordinary efforts during a winter of industrial depression, putting his pride in his pocket and taking laborer's work, which he had never done before. He finally got a good position and saved money enough to begin housekeeping. The probation officer kept in touch with the wife, first persuading her to receive a letter from Mr. Long and answer it through the probation office. He interested her in the details of her husband's struggle, and finally, after a whole year of probation and with the help of her pastor, he induced her to return. The probation officer kept in close touch with the family for some months and reports: "Three years have elapsed since that time; the family is now in a nearby city where they are living harmoniously and in comfortable circumstances."

A case worker who is remarkable for her suc-

BROKEN HOMES

cess in the treatment of estranged couples, when asked how she did it answered laconically, "talks and talks and talks." A study of her case records, however, shows certain points that recur again and again in her treatment.

She encourages man and wife, separately, to talk out their grievances thoroughly and get everything out of their systems. She then proceeds (with a lavish expenditure of time, as indicated in her phrase) to convince each that she is a friend, but an impartial friend. She does not push for an immediate reconciliation, is much more likely to recommend a temporary separation until tempers cool down and the true facts appear. She always advises strongly against "argument" and "casting up" the past, and tells the couple to come back to her if they want to discuss their grievances further. Above all, they are not to retail their troubles to relatives and friends. If either or both are out of the city during their separation she keeps in close touch with them by letter. She is quick to utilize their interest in their children as a means of reawakening their interest in each other. The

THE DETAILS OF TREATMENT

following letters illustrate her method. The first was written to a young man who was serving a six months' sentence for desertion; the others to the same young man after he had begun a manful struggle to "come back," working in a munitions plant in another state and later sending money regularly to the wife, who still obdurately refused to forgive him. (The letters are part of a series of 27 which were written to him during a ten months' period.)

My dear Mr. Andrews:

I was ever so glad to get your letter this week and I am sorry that no one has been over [to the workhouse] to see you recently. I will surely be over within the next two weeks. I know you are anxious and you should have had a letter telling you about the children. They are both all right now and the baby is out of the hospital.

We have had a nice talk with your aunt and she is very anxious to come over and see you. We will all get together and try and plan what is the right thing to do when you come out. I will arrange it so we can have a little longer talk this time if possible.

Very truly yours,
District Secretary.

My dear Mr. Andrews:

Your long letter has just arrived. I read it with a great deal of interest and pleasure. It is fine to know

BROKEN HOMES

you have already arrived and have started out to make good on your promises.

I got your cards during the week, which brought the news of your journey. Also on Tuesday morning came your last letter, expressing your appreciation for all we had tried to do for you and enclosing two more thrift stamps for the children. I put these in their books.

Yesterday I had a nice long letter from your father, enclosing one for me to give to you. I am sending it on just as it is. I was very much tempted to read it but have not done so. The reason I was tempted was that I know it must be full of happiness to think you have made such a good start. At least that was the tone of the letter he wrote to me.

During the past years I have worked for this society I have seen many people "come back" strong, and always it has been because they had some big motive in life and reason for making good. But I have seldom known a fellow that had so many reasons why he should make good. You have the confidence of your father and your aunt. You have the children for whom you will do right. You have Clara, whom you have wronged and whom you will have to teach all over again to trust you. Surely all these things added to your own firm will to try and undo all the unhappiness you have given people, ought to help you every day as you prove the good stuff that is in you.

I, of course, telephoned Clara of your starting off and yesterday she came to the office and we had a long talk. She is only sorry that you did not see the baby and says

THE DETAILS OF TREATMENT

she will be only too glad to have special pictures taken of the children to send you. This was after I suggested that she let me take a snapshot of them to send you.

Be sure and write to your father and aunt often. And please remember my last instructions, which were to let me know fully about yourself. When you write, tell me all about the camp life; how they arrange the living; how long hours you have to work; what they give you for recreation, etc. Pick out for your friends men who can help you, not hinder you, in your good determinations, and hope there will be at least one man there in whom you can trust and to whom you can go for advice.

I will let you know about the children all the time. Clara says Nellie [the small daughter] was expecting to see you again. Don't worry, she will never forget you.

With all good wishes,

Sincerely yours,

DISTRICT SECRETARY.

My dear Mr. Andrews:

I received your long letter this morning and was very glad to hear all the details of camp life. It is too bad that your surroundings are not more comfortable, but I am sure you can stick it out for awhile. If you can raise yourself to be foreman, will you then have to live in the same uncomfortable quarters? Although I don't know the details, I should think it would be well if you did sign up for the six months. It is too bad that your throat is still hoarse.

BROKEN HOMES

Thank you for letting me see your father's letter. I am enclosing it. I hope you are keeping in touch with him.

You asked especially about Clara and whether she asked for you. Of course she did, and she wants me to say if there is anything you want to say to her you can send the letter here and she will write you. She thinks that your ambition and determination to make good is fine, and she will try and help you in every way. She has not been in this week and I have been very busy, but I shall make it my business to see her early next week, and if she has not had the pictures of the children taken, I will get that attended to myself. . . .

So far as I can see there is absolutely nothing for you to worry about from this end of the line. Clara is at last, I think, as fully self-convinced as I am that you are making a splendid effort, and she is perfectly willing to be fair in waiting until you have a chance to get turned around financially and in making first payment for the children.

Next week I am going to send you down a book to read. It is one I have enjoyed myself, and perhaps some evenings when you are not too tired you will get a chance to glance over it. It is small and you can put it in your pocket. Be very sure I have not forgotten the very satisfactory talks we had and the splendid way you have grimly started out to make good. If you can help the Government do their work, even down there, give it a good try out: Never mind the different nationalities you have to mix with. You have already knocked

THE DETAILS OF TREATMENT

around the world so much that you can just consider this another opportunity of getting to know a great variety of people. You might even learn to talk Italian and Greek! There is no experience in life we have to go through but can be a source of great education to us. You are sure to win out and get the respect of everybody, your fellow-workmen as well as your superior officers, if you continuously day in and day out simply refuse to get discouraged and keep up your work and do as you are told. Stick by.

With all good wishes,

Sincerely yours,

DISTRICT SECRETARY.

But when all is said and done, there are no unbreakable rules about treatment. A form of treatment is sometimes to do nothing at all.

Charles Morgan, a middle-aged machinist with a wife, a comfortable home, and seven children (the two eldest grown), picked up his tools and disappeared, after a quarrel over his wife's extravagance. He had been earning $50 a week in a shop where he had worked for eighteen years and he would not endure having his wages garnisheed for debt.

An experienced case worker to whom furious Mrs. Morgan made her complaint, decided, after studying Mr. Morgan's record, that he ought not to be prosecuted, and refused to be party to it. As he was a man of domestic habits, search was made in a nearby city where he had

BROKEN HOMES

relatives. He was easily traced. Mr. Morgan was both proud and reticent, so the case worker made no attempt to approach him, but told the woman she must devise some way to get him back, preferably to write him and say she was sorry. This she refused to do and on her own responsibility adopted the clumsy device of wiring him that a favorite child was sick. This brought him "on the run," and, being back, he stayed. *The case worker has never seen Mr. M.*, nor has his wife been encouraged to come any more to the office, although reports have been received from time to time through the son and daughter that things at home continue to go well.

VIII

THE HOME-STAYING NON-SUPPORTER

MANY of the case workers consulted in gathering material for this book urged that a discussion of the treatment of the non-supporter who had not deserted be included in its pages. In so far as non-support is a pre-desertion symptom and the non-supporter a potential deserter, much that has been said applies also to him. But are the two groups co-terminous, or do they only partially overlap?

The law makes little difference in its treatment of the two, the fact of failure to support being the chief ground of its interest.* Indeed, in Massachusetts, the law under which deserters

* The deserter who does not fail to support is usually safe from punishment no matter how aggravated his offense. A man living with his wife and five-year-old boy in an eastern city eloped with another woman to a city in the Middle West. The couple kidnapped the boy and took him with them; and the distracted woman, bereft of both her husband and child, had no recourse in any court, since the father was continuing to provide for his son.

BROKEN HOMES

are extradited for abandonment is habitually spoken of as the "non-support law."

No study of which the results are available has been made to learn what difference, if any, exists between the non-supporter who leaves home and the one who does not. Miss Breed, in making the point that the true analogy of the deserted family is with the non-supported family and not with the widow and her children, says: "The deserting husband is at home the non-supporting husband."*

A case reader of experience writes: "When I look back over the many records I have read and studied, it seems to me that it is very difficult to draw a line between desertion and non-support cases, either in the kind of problem they present, or in the treatment of them. Do we know enough about non-supporters who later become deserters; and isn't it possible that every non-support case, certainly every beginning non-support case, is a potential desertion case?"

There is no doubt that the two groups grade imperceptibly into each other; but of the twenty or more case workers who were consulted in the

* Proceedings of the New York State Conference of Charities and Correction, 1910, p. 76.

THE HOME-STAYING NON-SUPPORTER

preparation of this material, nearly all felt that the out-and-out deserter, if he can be got hold of, is more promising material to work with than the man who sits about the home and lets others maintain it. They all recognize a common middle ground where the two groups merge into each other; but they see decided differences in the two "wings" so to speak, outside of this common ground.

Seen through their eyes, the non-supporter has less courage, initiative and aggressiveness than the deserter. "He is less deliberately cruel—for at least he 'sticks around.'" He has not the roving disposition, but is apt to be intemperate and industrially inefficient as compared with the deserter. Often the married vagabond, as he has been called, is a "home-loving man who simply shirks responsibility and dislikes effort." He may "sometimes feel parental responsibility even though he does not support," and he is likely to have less physical and mental stamina than the deserter. That phrase in which the psychiatrists take refuge, "constitutional inferiority," is more likely to

BROKEN HOMES

describe the stay-at-home than the wanderer. However, one social worker (non-medical) says "a mental twist more often enters into the problem of the deserter than into that of the non-supporter, from my experience."

The head of a large probation department writes: "Many of the deserters with whom we have dealt were non-supporters before coming to our attention. Among the men convicted of abandonment, however, is a group which is above the average in intelligence—skilled workers or men in professional occupations."

If this concurrence of observation is sound the reason for the social worker's preference for the deserter as material with which to work is not far to seek. With the deserter as described, the problem is chiefly to alter his point of view; with the non-supporter it is, in addition, to stiffen his will and to increase his capacity—a far more complicated task.

"The deserter is likely to have less justification than the non-supporter," says an observer of long experience. Studies which have been made of the relative capacity of the wives of deserters

THE HOME-STAYING NON-SUPPORTER

and of non-supporters seem to agree that the latter have the weaker characters and are less competent and successful workers. A comment made upon one such study points out the impossibility of sound conclusions, if both chronic and incipient cases are included in the two groups. The progressive demoralization in the family of the "intermittent husband" makes such a study of little value unless this distinction is taken into account.

The influence of ill-kept homes in the manufacture of non-supporting husbands has been widely recognized.

A drunkard's daughter, who had never known a decent home, married a young man who soon began to drink too. Luckily, the young couple were brought in touch with a volunteer visitor who, on finding that the wife possessed only two kitchen utensils, a teakettle and a "frypan," and actually did not know the names of any others, undertook to give her lessons in home management. She proved teachable, and her husband stopped drinking and braced up. Some years later the visitor was able to report a well established home, although the family refused to move out of the poor neighborhood in which they lived because the husband had been elected councilman for that district.

BROKEN HOMES

If the inefficient wife contributes her share to this form of family breakdown so also does the overefficient one. Many a non-supporter got his first impulse in that direction when his wife became a wage-earner in some domestic crisis. "There's only one rule for women who want to have decent homes for their children and themselves," advised a wise neighbor. "If your husband comes home crying, and says he can't find any work, sit down on the other side of the fire and cry until he *does*."*

One case worker comments on the relation that often exists between an inefficient husband and an unusually competent wife, made up of a motherly toleration on her side and a tacit acceptance on his that he is not expected to be the provider. "Sort of a landlady's husband" was the apt description of one such man, the speaker having in mind the "silent partner" who does odd jobs around his wife's furnished-room house. The lovable old rascal portrayed

---

* Loane, M.: The Queen's Poor, p. 102. London, Edward Arnold, 1905.

THE HOME-STAYING NON-SUPPORTER

by Frank Bacon in his play "Lightnin'" is typical of this kind of husband.

There is no ground for outside interference in such an arrangement as long as both are satisfied and the family as a unit is self-supporting. It is often a serious problem to the case worker, however, to know how to treat such a family if the breadwinner-wife becomes incapacitated. Such was the case when Mrs. Laflin fell ill with tuberculosis. Her relatives described her husband as "that little nonentity of a man." He had no bad habits and was pathetically eager to work, but though only a little over fifty he was prematurely aged and incapable. The solution had finally to be institutional care for the entire family, Mrs. Laflin in a hospital for incurables, Mr. Laflin in a home for the aged, and their two young daughters, through the interest of a former employer, in a good convent school. "Uncomplicated" non-support, as in the case of Mr. Laflin, is, however, rare in the experience of the social worker.

Out of a group of 51 non-supporters selected at random from the records of the Buffalo

BROKEN HOMES

Charity Organization Society in 1917, 46 showed some serious moral fault other than non-support. Alcoholism is probably the commonest of these complications; and, as has been pointed out in the previous chapter, is probably a primary cause as well. It will be a matter of great interest to social workers whether the "non-support rate" is reduced after July 1, 1919. Grounds for hope that it may be are found in the fact that some remarkable results have been obtained by moving alcoholic non-supporters and their families from "wet" into "dry" territory.

Another vice that has a direct relation to non-support (much more direct than to desertion) is gambling. The gambler carries no signs of his vice upon his person as does the inebriate, and it is therefore hard to detect. It undoubtedly does not appear in social case records as frequently as it should. Case workers should have it in mind as a possible explanation, whenever there is a marked discrepancy between what a non-supporter earns and what he contributes to the home.

With the non-supporters rather than with the

THE HOME-STAYING NON-SUPPORTER

deserters should be put the group of men whose wives tire of supporting them and either put them out or leave them. These men are often not only morally, but mentally and physically, so handicapped that there is nothing to be gained by constantly pursuing and arresting them, although some wives extract the sweets of revenge from doing just this. Few courts of domestic relations are without some wives as regular patrons who pursue their husbands not for gain but for sport. For the most part, however, the wives of such men are philosophical. "I only wash for meself now," said one of them.

These men, and the unreclaimed deserters, doubtless make up a large part of the floating population of homeless men in our large cities. How large a part it is impossible to say, for they are likely to give assumed names and deny the possession of families. Mrs. Solenberger* has noted, however, that if they are asked, not "Are you married?" but a less direct question such as "Where is your wife now?" a story of

* Solenberger, Alice Willard: One Thousand Homeless Men, p. 22. New York, Russell Sage Foundation, 1911.

BROKEN HOMES

unfortunate married life will often be elicited. Until we have some better method of inter-city registration of homeless men, many of these who otherwise might be identified and in suitable cases brought back, will continue to slip through our fingers.

With non-support in an incipient stage,* it is sometimes possible to deal so suddenly and effectively that the man is shocked into a better realization of his responsibilities.

A young Irish rigger, with a capable wife and two pretty babies, lost his job after a quarrel with his boss rigger. He was a genial, popular chap, always "the life of the party" in his circle; and his companions encouraged him to feel that he was a much injured man. They also helped him to fill his enforced leisure with too much beer. When the family received a dispossess notice the wife's patience was at an end, and acting on the advice of a society engaged in family case work, she put the furniture in storage and went to a shelter where she could leave her children in the daytime, while she was at work, and have them with her at night. The man was told to shift for himself until he could get together

* For a consideration of possible lines of treatment for the non-supporter and his family, the reader is referred to Chapter VII, where is discussed the treatment of the deserter who is willing to return.

THE HOME-STAYING NON-SUPPORTER

sufficient money to re-establish the home. The arrangement continued for nearly two months, during which the man lived in lodging houses, had an attack of stomach trouble, and was altogether thoroughly miserable. Every night he waited for a word with his wife on a corner that she had to pass in coming from work. Finally, when it seemed to the social worker and to the wife that his lesson had gone far enough, the home was re-established, with only a small amount of help from the society. During the five years since that time, no recurrence of the trouble has come to the attention of the agency interested.

This experiment was realized to be a ticklish one, as a man less sincerely attached to his home might have been turned into a vagabond by such treatment.

In general, it may be said that, as there is less to work on constructively with the non-supporter, court action has more often to be invoked. If the non-supporter is a "chronic," his path must not be allowed to be too easy. "Sometimes you just have to keep pestering him" was the way one social worker put it. A Red Cross Home Service worker successfully shocked one elderly non-supporter into going to work, as described in one of the Red Cross publications:

BROKEN HOMES

"Well, Mr. Gage," I said, "I see you're not working yet."

"No, Mrs. Cox, the coal company promised to send for me."

"Well," I said, "I think you've been pretty fair with that company. You've waited on it for three months now. If I had the offer of another job I'd feel perfectly free to take it, if I were you."

"Yes," he said, "I think I should."

"All right, I have a job for you," said I. "My husband wants a man now at his garage, to clean automobiles. The hours are from 6 p.m. to 6 a.m., and you'll earn $15 a week."

His paper fell from his hands to the floor; his jaw dropped, and he just looked at me. Then he tried to crawl out of it and began to make excuses.

"I haven't time to argue with you, Mr. Gage," I said. "I'll keep the job open till seven o'clock tonight and you can let me know then whether you'll take it or not."

At seven he came to say he'd take the job.[*]

If in desertion cases the interest centers very vividly about the absent man, in non-support cases the reverse is likely to be true, because he is often not very interesting per se, and because, moreover, he is always on the spot and does

[*] Behind the Service Flag, pamphlet ARC 211, American Red Cross, Department of Civilian Relief.

THE HOME-STAYING NON-SUPPORTER

not have to be searched for. Familiarity certainly breeds contempt for the non-supporter. Consequently the social worker may easily fall into the danger of disregarding the human factors he presents, and either treating the family as if he did not exist or expending no further effort on him than to see that he "puts in" six months of every year in jail if possible (since the law usually secures to him the privilege of loafing the other six). It is not safe, however, to regard even the most leisurely of non-supporters as beyond the possibility of awakening. One district secretary who had thus given a man up had the experience of seeing him transformed into a steady worker after a few months of intensive effort by a first-year student in a school of social science, whose only equipment for the job was personality and enthusiasm. So remarkable are some of the reclamations that have been brought about with seemingly hopeless non-supporters that all possible measures should be tried before giving one of them up.

His Scotch ancestry, a good wife, luck, and a friend with insight and skill, pulled Aleck Gray out of that

BROKEN HOMES

bottomless pit, the gutter. Aleck had been a bookkeeper; but he didn't get on well with his employers, lost his job, got to drinking, and went so far downhill that his wife had to take their two children and go home to her people several hundred miles away. Aleck finally drifted into a bureau for homeless men, where the agent became interested in him and worked with him for six months, getting him job after job, which he always lost through drink or temper. He seemed incapable of taking directions or working with other people. In all that time the agent felt that he was getting no nearer the root of Aleck's trouble, though he came back after each dismissal and doggedly took whatever was offered. Finally, the agent's patience wore thin, and when Aleck had been more than usually dour and aggravating it went entirely to pieces. Aleck listened to his outburst apparently unmoved; then said, "Very well, if you want to know what would make me stop drinking, I'll tell you. If I could see any ray of hope that I was on the way to getting my home and family back, I'd stop and stop quick." On the agent's desk there happened to be a letter from a friend who wanted a tenant farmer. He thrust it into Aleck's hand saying, "There's your chance if you mean what you say." The man's reply was to ask when he could get a train. At the end of several weeks Aleck wrote that he had not drunk a drop and was making good, which was enthusiastically confirmed by his employer. He begged the agent to intercede with his wife, and a letter went to her which brought the telegraphic reply, "Starting tomorrow."

THE HOME-STAYING NON-SUPPORTER

How they got through the first winter the agent never knew exactly. But they pulled through and the next year was easy, as country-born Aleck's skill came back. Six years later, during which time the agent heard from them once or twice a year, Aleck was still keeping straight, the children were doing well in school, and the family, prosperous and happy, had bought a farm of their own in another state.

IX

NEXT STEPS IN CORRECTIVE TREATMENT

ANY discussion of laws, their application, and enforcement, must perforce be very general, since the different states vary greatly in laws governing desertion and in equipment for their enforcement. Suggestions for a uniform federal desertion law are not considered here; the term "next steps" should be read as meaning not plans in actual prospect but rather the increase in legal facilities desirable from the social worker's point of view. In communities where no such facilities exist, social workers are in a good position to collect illustrative material and push for desirable changes in law and law enforcement. Especially advantageous is the position of the legal social agencies such as legal aid societies and special bureaus and committees for increasing the efficiency of the courts, many

NEXT STEPS IN CORRECTIVE TREATMENT

of which are affiliated with or maintained by the large family work societies.

1. Measures for the Discovery, Extradition or Deportation of the Deserter.—The nation-wide registration of males between certain ages, under the Selective Service Act, was widely utilized by social workers in finding deserting men, with the hearty co-operation usually of the draft boards. This fact forms no argument for universal registration as it was carried on in Germany before the war; no system which meant such cumbersome machinery or so much interference with the freedom of the individual ought to be advocated for a moment if it were solely for the purpose of keeping track of the small percentage of citizens who wish to evade their responsibilities, marital and other. Even such a non-military device as that which obligates every person to register successive changes of address with the postal authorities to facilitate delivery of mail would be contrary to the American spirit and easily evaded by people interested in concealing their whereabouts, unless enforced with all the

BROKEN HOMES

rigor of the European police system. But though we can advocate no system of manhood registration, we can avail ourselves of the incidental benefits of any that may be in force.

The Federal Employment Service offers a promising means of help in discovering the movements of deserters whose trade and probable destination are known. It should be entirely possible to work out a system by which the managers of the local employment bureaus should be furnished with name, description, copy of photograph, and so on, of a deserter who is being sought, so that the man if recognized could be traced or quickly apprehended if a warrant is already in the hands of the local police authorities. It may even be possible, under the federal employment service, to develop the long wished for national registration of casual and migratory labor. Need for some such system has been felt by all agencies trying to deal constructively with vagrants and homeless men. Little track can be kept not only of the individual wanderer but of the ebb and flow of the tides of "casual labor" without some system of

NEXT STEPS IN CORRECTIVE TREATMENT

this sort. If employment bureaus were required to forward to a central registry the names and some identifying particulars of every non-resident who applied for employment, the problem of finding the deserter would be rendered ten times easier than it is now.

One present obstacle to this and other improvements is the attitude of authorities—city, state, and federal—toward wife desertion. We have already mentioned the way in which the task of tracing the deserter has been thrust back upon the wife and the social worker, as if he were not an offender against the community as well as against his wife and children. Almost as widespread is the reluctance of the proper authorities to arrest the deserter and bring him back after he has been found. A general atmosphere of indifference and despair of accomplishing anything worth while surrounds any attempt to push the prosecution of a man who has taken refuge outside the community. Hope for the future lies in socializing the point of view of court officials, police, and district attorneys—a process in which the social worker must play a

BROKEN HOMES

large part. No chance should be lost to drive home the social and economic waste involved, by using the illustrative material which abounds in the files of most case work agencies.

The pernicious system by which the wife is required to serve summons and warrant upon the offending husband who is still in the same city, should be done away with entirely. The social agency, public or private, which has had to support or assist the man's family ought to be able to prefer a charge for non-support, and to take out a summons or a warrant and serve it without the wife's being present. The agency should in this case protect itself by securing from the wife a signed affidavit and authorization to act in her behalf. It may seem unimportant whether the wife makes such complaint in the court or to a private society. The psychological effect upon the man is, however, very different. If his wife initiates the complaint in court, his resentment is directed toward her—a fact which renders reconciliation more difficult if this is later attempted. In other cases, for the wife to make the complaint puts her in actual physical danger

NEXT STEPS IN CORRECTIVE TREATMENT

from the vindictive husband. If he is brought into court on the complaint of a social agency, part of that resentment at least is transferred to the intrusive social worker, who is not usually seriously troubled thereby and is far better able to bear the weight of the husband's displeasure than is his poor wife.

The absence of any treaty with Great Britain by which family deserters can be extradited to or from Canada makes the Dominion a place of refuge for many American evaders of family responsibilities. The National Conference of Charities and Correction,* at its meeting in Cleveland in 1912, passed a resolution on the need for such a treaty. As a result, largely through the efforts of Mr. William H. Baldwin, the treaty was signed and sent to the Senate for ratification in December, 1916. It was referred to the Committee on Foreign Relations, where it met with objection and has remained without action up to the present. The National Conference of Jewish Charities, at its meeting

* Now changed to The National Conference of Social Work.

BROKEN HOMES

in Kansas City in May, 1918, sent urgent representations to the Senate Committee, which it is hoped may result in ratification after the pressure of war-time legislation is relaxed.

We should not stop when reciprocal extradition with Canada has been secured; there is a similar situation on our southern border in states from which escape into Mexico is easy. While American deserters are not likely to go to other more remote countries than these two, immigration into America from other countries creates desertion problems in other places and presents us with a class of undesirables with whom it is difficult to deal under existing immigration laws. In 1912 a report was submitted to the Glasgow Parish Council showing the alarming amount of dependency created in that one city by the emigration to America and the Colonies of men without their families, and who subsequently drifted into the status of deserters. This report makes the interesting suggestion that no married man be permitted to emigrate without his family unless he presents a "written sanction of the Parish Council or other local

NEXT STEPS IN CORRECTIVE TREATMENT

authority," and further, that he be bound, under penalty of deportation, to report himself to some authority in the country of his destination, which would satisfy itself as to his conduct and insure that he did his duty by wife and family.*
Such a provision would of course involve the revision of our own immigration laws, making wife and family desertion a crime thereunder.

At present the law provides deportation only within five years after entry, and for "persons who have been convicted of or admit having committed a felony or other crime or misdemeanor involving moral turpitude," or who are sentenced to a term of one year or more in this country, within five years of entry, for such crime (or who may suffer a second conviction at any time after entry). This would clearly cover bigamy committed within five years after entry; whether it could be stretched to cover lesser forms of marital irresponsibility remains to be determined. (It should be remembered

* Motion, J. R.: Wife and Family Desertion: Emigration as a Contributory Cause. Glasgow Parish Council, 1912.

BROKEN HOMES

that a man who brings in as his wife, or later sends for, a woman to whom he is not married, can be deported under quite other sections of the immigration law.)

2. Improvements in Court Procedure.—A sore point with the social worker is the often ridiculously inadequate amounts that unwilling husbands are put under court order to pay. They accuse the courts, whether rightly or wrongly, of considering first what part of the man's alleged earnings will be needed for him to live upon comfortably, and then of making the order for whatever may be left over.

Onofrio Mancini was under court order to stay away from home and pay his wife $6.00 a week for the support of their two children. He drove a two-horse truck, and, at that time, must have been earning not less than $16.00 a week. Mrs. Mancini fell ill, whereupon Onofrio promptly ceased all payments. The social agency interested was permitted to make a complaint on producing a doctor's certificate that Mrs. Mancini could not appear in court; but Onofrio, when he appeared, put up such a hard luck tale of earning only $8.00 a week that the judge, without investigation, cut the order down to $4.00 a week and *ordered Onofrio to return home to live*.

NEXT STEPS IN CORRECTIVE TREATMENT

A bulletin issued by the Seybert Institution of Philadelphia gives a very interesting set of diagrams showing the relation (or lack of relation) between the amount of man's income, size of family, and the court order issued in the Philadelphia Municipal Court.*

This report gives a series of illustrations, where glaring inconsistencies between the man's earnings and the court order were observed by visitors to the court. A sample of the reports made by these visitors is as follows:

"Man earning $30 to $40 a week at ammunition factory. Can earn $20 with no overtime. Has been sending woman $10 a week but has threatened to leave town. Judge said: 'You can't keep up $10 a week—how much can you give?' Finally ordered $8 a week. Woman said she couldn't live on that and Judge told her she had to go to work herself then; that they should live together anyway. Woman says she is unable to work—is ill. When man stated he was giving $10 great consternation seemed to take hold of the entire court force. He

* Handling of Cases by the Juvenile Court and Court of Domestic Relations of the Philadelphia Municipal Court. Bulletin 2, Bureau for Social Research, the Seybert Institution, Philadelphia, 1918.

BROKEN HOMES

did not say he couldn't pay $10; the judge simply told him he couldn't keep that up."

The practice of assigning less than half the man's weekly earnings to the wife and children has been defended on the ground that if he is forced to live too economically, he will disappear and the family will be left with nothing. This would seem to be a self-confession on the part of the court that it cannot enforce its reasonable requirements. It would appear that the first thing to be considered is the minimum needs of the wife and children, taking into consideration whether the wife can be expected to contribute anything toward her own support or whether all her time is needed for her children. This amount should be cut down only when there is actually not enough left for the man to live on; and his wife and children should not be pinched for necessities in order that he may have luxuries or indulge in vices. The habit some judges have of accepting the man's own statement on oath as to what his earnings are is responsible for many unjust orders. A man who does not want to contribute to his family's

NEXT STEPS IN CORRECTIVE TREATMENT

support is almost sure to understate his earnings, oath or no oath; and the confirmation of his employer (or when the employer is suspected of being in league with him, the inspection of the employer's books by the probation officer) is often needed. Probably the most difficult form of evasion to combat is that of the man who deliberately takes a lower salary than he is capable of earning, so as to have less to give his wife. Surprising as it may seem, this is a common practice; but skilful probation work can nevertheless find a remedy.

In cases of suspended sentence, payments ought always to be made through the court and not handed by the man to his wife. It is better to have the amount received and transmitted by some bureau attached to the court, and so managed that the man can send the money in without "knocking off work" to bring it and that the woman can receive it by mail. The probation officer should not be bothered with the actual handling of the money, but he should be promptly notified of any delinquency in the payments.

BROKEN HOMES

Whether the man under court order is on probation or not, the cessation of payments should automatically reopen the case. At present, in most courts, the order goes by default until the wife comes in to make another charge. This, through discouragement or fear of a beating from the man, she often neglects; with the result that the orders of the court mean little in the eyes of the men, and that arrears, once allowed to mount up, are never cleared off.

This statement applies as well to long term orders for separate support where the circumstances are such that no reconciliation is contemplated. These orders are now made for a definite period of months, at the end of which time the case drops unless the wife renews charges. A case of this sort ought not to be terminable without a reinvestigation and final hearing in court. Indeed it would seem, in such cases, that the children involved should have at least as much protection as the children in bastardy proceedings, and that the order should be made to cover the term of years until the oldest child becomes of working age.

NEXT STEPS IN CORRECTIVE TREATMENT

The most important step in advance with regard to payments is undoubtedly the law which has been tried with signal success in the District of Columbia and in the states of Ohio and Massachusetts, requiring men serving prison sentences for non-support and abandonment to be made to work, and a sum of money, representing their earnings, to be turned over to their families.

In an interesting paper in the *Survey* for November 20, 1909, entitled "Making the Deserter Pay the Piper," Mr. William H. Baldwin discusses in detail how this plan was made to work successfully in the District of Columbia.

The movement for special courts to consider cases of juvenile delinquency and marital relations has gained such headway that no word needs to be said here in its favor. In communities where the volume of court business permits such courts to be separately organized, they are generally accepted as the only means of handling these matters. In smaller communities the need may be met by setting aside regular sessions of the magistrates' courts for this purpose.

BROKEN HOMES

Juvenile courts and domestic relations courts having proved a success separately, there is a strong movement on foot to combine them into one court, for which the name Family Court has been proposed.

A leader in this movement is Judge Hoffman of the Family Court of Cincinnati, which he describes thus:

"The Court of Cincinnati was organized for the purpose of dealing with the family as a unit and to ascertain possibly the cause of its disruption. It has exclusive jurisdiction in all divorce and alimony cases, and all matters coming under the Juvenile Court Act. It also has jurisdiction in cases of failure to provide. The ideal court would include in connection with the foregoing functions, adoption of children, the issuing of marriage licenses, and bastardy cases."[*]

One advantage of this plan is the economy it effects in the time of probation officers. It is generally admitted that in children's court cases it is the parents rather than the children who are really on probation; and with two courts and two separate probation systems, we may

[*] Hoffman, Charles W.: The Domestic Relations Court and Divorce, *The Delinquent*, February, 1917.

NEXT STEPS IN CORRECTIVE TREATMENT

even have the anomaly of the same family being under the care of two probation officers at once. Specialization can no further go! Other leaders in the domestic relations court movement see little merit in the proposal for a one-part family court. They think that, in the large cities at least, the need would be better served by having the domestic relations and juvenile courts under one roof, but as two separate and distinct parts of the same court. All are agreed, however, that the powers of one or the other of the two special courts should be enlarged to cover bastardy cases, where this is not now done.

The domestic relations court, whether separate or as part of a family court, ought to have equity powers, so that the usual rules of evidence need not be so closely adhered to and more latitude could be allowed the magistrate in disposing of cases, not necessarily according to ruling and precedent but according to the social needs disclosed. A constitutional amendment now pending in New York is a model for this sort of legislation. It is in part as follows:

BROKEN HOMES

"The legislature may establish children's courts and courts of domestic relations as separate courts or parts of existing courts, or courts hereafter to be created, and may confer upon them such equity and other jurisdiction as may be necessary for the correction, protection, guardianship and disposition of delinquent, neglected or dependent minors, and for the punishment and correction of adults responsible for or contributing to such delinquency, neglect or dependency, and to compel the support of a wife, child or poor relative by persons legally chargeable therewith who abandon or neglect to support any of them."*

Many courts of domestic relations which now exercise equity powers, such as ordering that a man remain away from home or that a wife allow her husband to see his children at stated times, do so without actual legal warrant and subject at any time to appeal of counsel. The conferring of equity powers on courts of domestic relations is a form of protection both to the court and to its clients which social workers should stand ready to work for.

Juvenile courts have in the main outstripped

* For a fuller discussion of equity powers see an article by Judge C. F. Collins in the *Legal Aid Review* for January, 1919.

NEXT STEPS IN CORRECTIVE TREATMENT

the domestic relations courts in the use of physicians and psychiatrists. The best examples of both these courts have, however, facilities for the making of physical examinations and mental tests, where necessary, before adjudication. Judge Hoffman says that the fact that so many cases in courts of domestic relations disclose abnormal or perverted sex habits, makes important the services of a psychiatrist accustomed to diagnosing these conditions.*

In most states the jurisdiction of the courts of domestic relations should be extended and co-ordinated. Few states escape some glaring inconsistencies in the laws governing desertion and abandonment. There is, for instance, much confusion between states as to whether a woman whose husband brings her to a strange city and there deserts her must prosecute him in the city where their home is or where the desertion took place. Under certain circumstances the woman is forced to travel to the city where her husband has gone, and bring action against him there,

* Hoffman, Charles W.: Domestic Relations Courts and Divorce. *The Delinquent*, February, 1917.

BROKEN HOMES

if the courts in that place will entertain a suit. In New York state there is no law which covers the case of a man who abandons his wife while she is pregnant, if there is no other living child. To constitute an extraditable crime there must have been abandonment of a child *in esse* not merely *in posse*.

But no institution, however carefully established by law, is any more effective than the people who run it; and the usefulness of the domestic relations court in any community depends entirely upon the social-mindedness and freedom from political entanglement of the judge and the amount and quality of probation service. From a social point of view, the latter is more important than the former; for a bad decision of the court can be mitigated by good case work later on, while a poor probation officer may nullify the effects of the wisest judicial decision ever made.

The importance of having enough probation officers to handle the work of the court has already been touched upon. An overworked officer is perforce an inefficient officer. He has

NEXT STEPS IN CORRECTIVE TREATMENT

usually to spend at least half his time in the court and attending to the clerical end of his job. From 50 to 60 cases is probably all that one probation officer can be expected to handle thoroughly at one time, if, as is to be hoped, he is required to make careful preliminary investigations to be presented to the judge *before* the trial.

In training and in equipment for the job, probation officers should be the equals of case workers in private agencies. Examinations for probation officers ought to be conducted by social workers of skill and high standards. A few months of cramming at a civil service school, or a few weeks of volunteer visiting with some case working agency, should not suffice to enable candidates to pass the examinations. The standards should be high enough and the salaries sufficiently attractive to draw into this field people who have successfully completed their apprenticeship in the art of case work. Only then can the status of the probation officer be raised to what it should be in the court itself. The relation of the probation officer to the judge

BROKEN HOMES

ought to be exactly like the relation of the medical social worker to the physician—that of a person acting under his direction in a general way, but with a special contribution to make to the treatment of the case and with a recognized standing as an expert in his own particular field.

X

NEXT STEPS IN PREVENTIVE TREATMENT

AT this time of writing it is too soon after the signing of the armistice to make predictions as to what the Great War may do to marriage. Whether desertion and divorce will increase or decrease it is impossible to say, and the experience of Europe is beside the mark. The war will leave traces on this generation—no doubt about that; but our losses have not been heavy enough seriously to disturb the balance of the sexes. The war, which has been to the common people of our country a war of service and ideals, has erased much that was petty and selfish; it has also caused nervous shocks and strains incalculable and unimagined. Years from now we may be able to strike the balance, but today this cannot be done. It is impossible also to say whether the growing

BROKEN HOMES

irresponsibility that was generally recognized to be threatening married life in the years before the war is still operating with like effect, or whether the full tide of emotion in which the world has been lately submerged may have swept at least a part of it away.

We are dealing here, however, not so much with modifications in the spirit of the times, as with prevention in the individual case.

One very fundamental claim can be made concerning marital shipwrecks; namely, that the way to prevent many of them would have been to see that the marriage never was allowed to take place. Marriage laws and their enforcement form a whole subject in themselves which is now receiving careful study, the results of which should be available shortly.* This fact precludes any discussion of the subject here, though the relation of our marriage laws to marital discord is so obvious that some mention of the matter is necessary.

---

* See, for example, American Marriage Laws in their Social Aspects—a preliminary study by the Russell Sage Foundation, June, 1919.

NEXT STEPS IN PREVENTIVE TREATMENT

It was formerly the belief of students of family desertion that the best way to prevent desertions was to punish them quickly and severely. It should be said that this plan has never received a fair trial on a large scale, for legal equipment has always lagged behind knowledge. It may be true that just as a community can, within limits, regulate its death rate by what it is willing to pay, so it can by repressive measures regulate its desertion rate. But measures that keep the would-be deserter in the home which constantly grows less of a home, simply through fear of consequences if he left it, seem hardly a desirable form of prevention from the social point of view. It would be much better to catch the disintegrating family in whatever form of social drag-net could be devised, and deal with it individually and constructively along the lines which case work has laid down.

Is it possible, however, to recognize a "pre-desertion state?" And if so, what are the danger signals? One case worker answers this question sententiously: "Any influences which tend to destroy family solidarity are possible signs of

BROKEN HOMES

desertion." Another writes: "We have sometimes found it possible to recognize a 'pre-desertion state' in the intermittent deserter, where we know the conditions which previously led to desertion, but I doubt whether we have very often been able to note it in the case of first desertions. In general, I should say a growing carelessness or a growing despondency as to his ability to care for his family are danger signals in the man, of which it is well to keep track."

The conditions listed in Chapter II as "contributory factors" might in certain combinations be decided danger signals of impending desertion. Non-support itself is, indeed, one of the most common of such signals, though a man who has dealt with hundreds of desertion cases maintained recently that the best and most hopeful type of deserter is the one who supports his family adequately up to the time of leaving home.

In the following case the items that led the case worker to suspect an approaching desertion are set down in the order stated by her. The

NEXT STEPS IN PREVENTIVE TREATMENT

couple were Irish; the man had never deserted before.

(1) He had spoken with eagerness of the wages that were being earned in munition plants in a city a few hours away—said he would like to go to some of those munition places and see what he could make.

(2) He was an intermittent drinker.

(3) His work record was poor; employers said he was irregular and unreliable.

(4) Visitor felt he had never earned as much as he was easily capable of earning and was rather indifferent to the needs of his family.

(5) The woman was willing to work—had applied for day nursery care, but visitor had persuaded the nursery not to accept the children.

After the visitor had stated the first two of the above items she stopped, and did not add the more significant three that followed until reminded that many workmen who drank intermittently were at that time thinking enviously of munition factory wages; and that these hardly constituted danger signals. The cumulative effect of all five items cannot, however, be denied.

Another statement, similarly obtained, con-

BROKEN HOMES

cerns a colored couple, married about two years and with two children, the youngest less than a month old. Man had been out of work and family had gone to live with relatives.

(1) Man earns $20 a week but refuses to start housekeeping again, although they are seriously overcrowded—seven adults and five children in five rooms.

(2) Woman says he makes her sleep on chairs so that he can get better rest.

(3) He is seeing a good deal of another woman, a friend of the wife (wife's statement only).

(4) Woman had applied for nursery care for both children so that she might go to work.

(5) It transpires that she lived with him before marriage, and that the first child was a month old when the marriage took place. He "holds it over her."

(6) Man had been married before and divorced.

(7) The family's habits of recreation are changed; the man no longer "takes her out."

Such attempts to foretell the future are not infallible, of course; but a listing process is a valuable aid to diagnosis, and, by its help, a situation may be uncovered which tends toward complete family breakdown. This may be taken in time and prevented; or, if separation is inevitable it can be prepared for in advance, the

NEXT STEPS IN PREVENTIVE TREATMENT

necessary legal arrangements can be made to protect the family, and the anxiety, suspense, and useless effort avoided which a sudden and downright abandonment would cause.

But the trouble is that the problem seldom comes to the case worker until matters have progressed farther than this. The real question is—not how to recognize pre-desertion symptoms, but how to get hold of families when these symptoms are in the incipient stage.

Mr. Hiram Myers, manager of the Desertion Bureau of the New York Association for Improving the Condition of the Poor, who has made a close study of the subject, holds the theory that the real period of stress in marital adjustment comes not during the "critical first year," about which we have been told so much, but at a later period, which he sets roughly at from the third to the fifth year after marriage. By this time there are usually one or two babies, the wife's girlish charm has gone, and the romance of the first attraction has vanished, while the steady force of conjugal affection which should smooth their path through the years

BROKEN HOMES

ahead has not come to take its place. It is in this middle period that longings for the delights of his care-free youth begin to come back to a man; if he ever had the wandering foot, it begins again to twitch for the road; or else his fancy is captured by some other girl not tied down at home by children. It is at this time, too, that endless discords and misunderstandings arise—that the last bit of gilt crumbles off the gingerbread.

As a result of his observations, Mr. Myers feels sure that the majority of first desertions take place somewhere from the third to the fifth year after marriage. Miss Brandt's[*] careful statistical study of 574 deserted families shows that in nearly 46 per cent of the families the first desertion took place before the fifth year of married life. Of course the jars that may come in the earlier months of marriage are seldom brought to the attention of social agencies, as it is usually the presence of children in the family and the consequent burden upon the

[*] Brandt, Lilian: 574 Deserters and their Families, p. 23. Charity Organization Society of New York, 1905.

NEXT STEPS IN PREVENTIVE TREATMENT

wife which make such agencies acquainted with her.

It is to be hoped that further study will be made upon these points. It is well known and accepted that the majority of first deserters are young men; but if certain danger periods in married life can be definitely recognized, many new possibilities in prevention and treatment will be opened up.

A number of experiments and suggestions have lately been made which may prove to be the means of recognizing marital troubles early. The probation department of the Chicago Court of Domestic Relations some years ago established a consultation bureau to which people might come or be sent for advice on difficult matrimonial situations, and without any court record being made. The Department of Public Charities of New York City maintains a similar bureau which is, however, so closely connected with the court that its clients make little distinction between them.

In addition to such conscious efforts to reach out after marital tangles in the pre-court stage,

BROKEN HOMES

there has recently been an interesting though accidental development in the city of Cleveland. During the thrift campaign of 1918, several savings banks of that city conceived the idea that their depositors could be induced and helped to save more money if the banks opened a bureau for free advice to their patrons on household management. This bureau is still in the experimental stage but it has had an increasing clientele so far. One thing that has astonished its management—but which causes no surprise in the mind of a social worker—has been the great variety of problems other than those connected with the family budget that have come to light in the bureau's consultations. Particularly is this true of marital discord centering about money affairs.

If such bureaus prove their usefulness there is no reason why they might not be greatly extended, and why other agencies than banks (insurance companies, for example) might not be eager thus to serve their customers. This opens a new field for the home economist, but incidentally it would appear that, in order to func-

NEXT STEPS IN PREVENTIVE TREATMENT

tion successfully, such bureaus would need to have access to the services of agencies employing highly skilled social case workers. It is conceivable that, if there are developed in our large cities consultation facilities under social auspices for people who feel their marriages going wrong, and want help and advice in righting them, such bureaus as those described above would be excellent "feeders" for this new form of social service.

Family social agencies have been distinctly backward in some of their approaches to the fundamental problems of family life. The failure of most of them, for instance, to study or seek improvements in the laws governing marriage or in their administration, is difficult of explanation. Such a consultation service as that suggested does, however, indicate a new point of departure in dealing with marital relations which would seem to fall distinctly within the field of the family case work agencies. It is time that these agencies began to find means of dealing, not with the dependent family alone but with the family in danger of becoming dependent—not with the family broken and estranged only, but with the one whose bonds, even if cracking and ill-adjusted, still hold.

Concretely, why should not family agencies establish such consultation bureaus as have just been mentioned, distinct from their regular activities and hampered by no suggestion in their title of association with problems of dependency? Dr. William Healy of Boston ascribes much of his success in getting the parents of defective and backward children to bring them voluntarily for examination to the fact that the name of his organization (the Judge Baker Foundation) conveys no hint of stigma or inferiority. Here is a valuable lesson in right publicity.

A bureau of family advice such as has been suggested should be under unimpeachable auspices from the point of view of medicine and psychiatry; it should have the services not only of expert social workers and experts in household management, but of doctors and psychiatrists as well. If it could be run as a joint-stock enterprise, in which courts and social agencies might be equally interested, so much the better. Its

NEXT STEPS IN PREVENTIVE TREATMENT

investigations should be searching enough to discourage applications from curiosity-mongers; but its services, like those of any clinic, should be given for whatever the patient is able to pay. Its relations, needless to say, should be entirely confidential, and as privileged in the eyes of the law as are those of doctor, lawyer, and priest.

It may be objected that people guard their marital infelicities too jealously and are too loath to discuss them to come willingly to such a place; that the idea involves a presumptuous interference in the private lives of individuals. But neurologists know that people in increasing numbers feel the need, under conditions of modern stress, for a safe outlet and a chance to discuss their perplexities and find counsel.

Fifty years ago the interest now taken by the social and medical professions in the question of whether mothers are rearing their infants properly could not have been foreseen. The establishment of baby health stations, or the activities of the Children's Bureau, would have been looked upon as unwarranted interference between the child and its mother, whose natural instincts could be depended upon to teach her how to nourish it. This point of view is no longer held; and the community's duty to take an interest in the upbringing of its children is never questioned. Is it not conceivable that, before another half century has rolled around, the community may take the same intelligent interest in the conservation of the family, and that definite efforts, which are now almost entirely lacking, may be made to stabilize and protect it?

Educational propaganda would, of course, have to be a definite part of the work of such bureaus. By this is meant not such modern specialties as "birth control," "sex hygiene," *et al.*, though we may by that time have enough authoritative information about sex psychology in marriage to be able to afford some help along these lines. Instruction in the *ethics* of married life and parenthood is of even more fundamental importance. The prevailing cynicism, the present low concepts of marriage, should be vigorously combatted by such an organization. Religious instruction would be, of course, beyond its

NEXT STEPS IN PREVENTIVE TREATMENT

scope; but it should be able to work sympathetically with all creeds, supplementing their teachings without seeking to duplicate them.

The services of such a bureau could not, of course, be forced upon anyone who did not wish to avail himself or herself of them; but definite though tactful efforts could be made to reach all young couples (just as are now being made to reach young mothers) with information as to where advice could be obtained.

No trustworthy figures exist as to the number of families broken by desertion or divorce in the United States, or as to the burden of actual dependency caused. Courts, probation officers, psychiatrists, and family case workers are all dissatisfied with our efforts to patch up the families which are already disintegrating. One of the three groups mentioned is likely before long to attempt some more dynamic attack upon the problem in its inception. If any suggestions herein contained find use in that program, the labor of compiling them will have been indeed well spent.

INDEX

Adolph R.: case story of, 69–70, 83

Age: relation of differences in, 27

Agencies: N. Y. Charity Organization Society, 44; National Desertion Bureau, 65, 69, 71, 101; United Hebrew Charities, 71; co-operative methods, 72–78, 84, 86–90; opinions on methods of arrest, 77, 78; N. Y. Association for Improving Condition of the Poor, 156, social problems and consultation bureaus, 195–199

Alcoholism: statistics on, 22; devastating effects of, 42; case story of woman, 57–61; and justifiable deserters, 111–114; relation to non-support, 156

American Marriage Laws in their Social Aspects, study by Russell Sage Foundation, 186

Apparent desertions: illustrated, 8, 9

Baldwin, Wm. H., 169, 177

Bastardy Cases, A Study of. Louise deK. Bowen, 95

Bastardy, see *Forced marriages*

Behind the Service Flag, Red Cross pamphlet, 160

Bigamy: and common law marriages, 98; immigrant deserters, 99

Bosanquet, Helen, 13

Bowen, Louise deK., 95

Brand, Harvey: case story of, 122

Brandt, Lilian, 16, 27, 192

Breed, Mary, 61, 150

Buffalo Charity Organization Society: non-support records, 156

Bureaus: National Desertion Bureau, 65, 69, 101; for consultation, 193–199; Court of Domestic Relations, Chicago, 193; Department of Public Charities, New York, 193; Children's Bureau, 197; importance of educational, 198–199. See also *Agencies*

Byington, Margaret F., 12

Canada: extradition treaties sought, 119, 169

Carstens, C. C., 68

Case illustrations: of apparent desertion, 8; mental deficiency, 24; reconciliation through education, 30; incompatibility and the "other woman," 40; interviewing the man essential, 57–61; liberal relief policy, 62; agency co-operation, 69, 75, 82, 83, 84; accident case, 79; traced through letter, 81; reconciliation after court marriage, 95; "American" marriages, 99; justifiable desertion, 111, 112–114; antagonism, 111–112; prison sentences helpful, 121, 122; adequate relief rids wife of chronic deserter, 131; adjustment impossible, 134; real affection a basis of

201

INDEX

reconciliation, 135; rehabilitation of a deserter, 137; wife reluctant to return to man who reformed, 141; non-support and ill-kept homes, 153; reestablishing non-supporters' homes, 158, 160, 161-163; inadequate court orders, 172, 173

Case work, see *Social workers*

Causal factors: analysis of study, 10, 15; motives and theories, 17-49; rationalization discussed, 17-22; summary of statistics, 21-22, 26-27, 45; feeble-mindedness, 24-25; training and self-control, 25-26; nationality, 26-27; religion, 27; age, 27; environment, 27-28; wrong basis of marriage 28; common law marriage, 29; ignorance, 29; incompetence, 31; wanderlust, 32; inadequate income, 32; financial mismanagement, 33; physical condition, 34-35; temperamental differences, 36; sex incompatibility, 37-39; vice and disease, 39-43; relatives, interference of, 43-44; racial studies, 44-45; community standards, 45-46; recreation, 47; companions, influence of, 48; shifting responsibility, 48; underlying causes, 49; seeking a working basis, 91-105

Charitable relief: desertion in expectation of, 48, 61; Mary Breed on, 61; immigrant's interpretation of, 99-100. See also *Collusion*

Chicago Court of Domestic Relations, bureau for marital advice, 193

Chicago Juvenile Protective Association: study of forced marriages by, 94-95

Children's Bureau, 197

Closing the case: extended treatment recommended, 63

Colcord, J. C., 61, 104, 133

Collins, C. F., 180

Collusion: infrequency of, 52, 70; case stories of, 71, 72; statistics of National Desertion Bureau, 71; preventive measures, 73-80

Common law marriages: legal protection under, 29; confusion of state laws, 98

Community ideals, see *Standards*

Companions: influence, and wanderlust, 47-48; aid in finding deserters, 77, 80

Co-operation of agencies, 68-78, 84, 86-90; suggested methods of finding deserters, 78-90; probation officers, 116, 122-124

Corrective treatment: legislative recommendations, 164-184; military systems aid in tracing deserters, 165-166; obstacles, 167; serving a warrant or summons, 168; extradition treaties recommended, 169; dependency through emigration, report on, 170; deportation laws, 171; court orders to pay, Seybert Institution report on, 172-177; special courts for juvenile delinquents, 177, 178, 179; Family Court of Cincinnati, 178; domestic relations court, 178, 179-180, 181-182; probation officers, 182-184

Court intervention: policy of treatment in past, 50-51; reasons, and laxity of laws, 51-52; social agency statistics, 52; a last resort, 53-54; effect of, 55, 95; for persistent deserters, 114-117; extradition, 117-119; probation, 119-124; warrant served by wife, 127; effecting reconciliations, 132-140; domestic relation courts effect reconciliations, 132; volunteers, 139-140; inadequacy of orders, 172-177; for juvenile delinquents, 178, 181; domestic relations, 179-182, 193

INDEX

Department of Public Charities, New York City, bureau of domestic relations, 193

Deserters and their Families, 574. Lilian Brandt, 192

Desertion and Non-Support in Family Case Work. Joanna C. Colcord, 61, 104, 133

Detectives: methods objectionable, 74, 77

Disease: statistical analysis, 22; and psychiatry, 24; effects of physical debility, 34; venereal disease, 41; alcoholism, 42. See also *Medical-Social work*

District of Columbia: non-support laws, 177

Divorce: relation to desertion, 7, 8; not considered, 16; administration of laws, and respect for, 46, by publication, 101; clearing bureau for, 101–102; for long continued desertion, 110; legal separation to protect wife, 127; bureaus might prevent, 193–199

Domestic relations courts: to combine with juvenile, 178, 179; Family Court of Cincinnati, 178; equity powers for, 179, 180; amendment pending, 179; facilities, 181

Domestic Relations Court and Divorce. C. W. Hoffman, 178, 181

Donald, Patrick: case story of, 19

Drug addiction, see *Narcotics*

Early influences: and self-control 25–26; educational, 29, 30, 46, 92, 153, 198

Economics: ratio of desertions in "hard times," 21, 32; family finances, 33; service bureaus, 194

Education: social studies of family life, 11–14; early training and delinquency, 26; background for failures, 29–30; destructive forces, 46; suggestions for case workers, 63; Attendance Department traces deserters, 73; non-support and inefficiency eliminated by, 153; propaganda, 198

Ellis, Havelock, 39

Environment: and immigration, 27–28; neighborhood standards, 46, 102

Equity powers, of domestic relations courts, 179, 180

Eubank. E. E., 21

Extradition: state problems, 117–119; for dangerous men, 129–130; non-support law. 150; treaties essential, ratification pending, 169, 170; N. Y. state law, 182

Extravagance: family finances, 33

Family as a Social and Educational Institution, The. Willystine Goodsell, 11

Family Court of Cincinnati, 178

Family Desertion. Lilian Brandt, 26

Family Desertion, A Study of. E. E. Eubank, 21

Family life: permanence of, 9, 11–15; spiritual values of, 12, 29; consultation service to solve problems of, 195–199

Family, The. Helen Bosanquet, 13

Fear of bodily harm from dangerous deserters, 128–129

Federal Employment Service, 166

Finding deserters, 65–90; National Desertion Bureau, 65, 69, 71; urgency of finding the

203

INDEX

man, 67; C. C. Carstens quoted, 68; example of, 69-70; collusion, instances of, 70-73; literature lacking, 74; detective methods, illustration of, 74-77; suggestions for, 78-80; through military authorities, 81-82; trade places, 82-83; publications, 83, 84, 85; bulletin boards, 84; employment agencies, 84; agency co-operation, 86-90

First desertions: temporary character of, 8; medical-social work a preventive, 9; accident records aid in tracing, 79; critical nature of, 91; when apt to occur, 191-192

First problem in desertion, 67, 91

Forced marriages: irregular unions, 28; investigation of, and statistics, 92-96; study by Chicago Juvenile Protective Association, 94; case illustrations, 95-96

Forel, August, 39

Francis, Mrs.: case story of, 131

Frost, Robert, 14

Gambling: effect upon character, 43; relation to non-support, 156

Glasgow Parish Council, report on dependency, 170-171

Goodsell, Willystine, 11

Gorokhoff, Andreas: case story of, 121

Gray, Aleck: case story of, 161-163

Hart, Bernard, 20

Healy, Dr. William, 196

Heredity: psychopathic personality, 24; feeble-mindedness, 25; racial differences, 26-28

Hoffman, Charles W., 178, 181

Illustrations, see *Case illustrations*

Immorality, see *Sex factors*

Inadequate relief: legal separation, and the law, 128; wife's attitude, 130; illustrated, 131; court orders, inconsistency of, 172-176; recent legislation to correct, 177. See also *Non-support*

Income: economic issues, 21, 22, 30; wages and non-support 32-33

Incompatibility: temperamental differences, 36; sex relations, 37-39, 40

Industrial deficiency: in husband and wife, 25, 31; national registration to correct, 166

Insanity: study of defectives, 20, 24

Insanity, The Psychology of Bernard Hart, 20

Instability: forms of, mental and physical, 17-22; factors that induce, 24-43, 47-49

"Intermittent husbands," 43, 153

Interviewing the man: importance of, 55-57, 105; case story, 57-61

Italy: marriage registration in 100

Judge Baker Foundation, of Boston, 196

Justifiable deserters: and alcoholism, 42; case illustration, 57-61, 111; procedure with, 112

Justification: thirst for experience, 9, 19; process of rationalization, 20; venereal disease and separation, 41; alcohol, and "justifiable deserters," 42; Williams case illustrates, 57-61, 111; and the non-supporter, 152-154

INDEX

Juvenile courts: movement for special, 177, 178; Juvenile Court Act, 178; combine with domestic relation courts, 178; Family Court of Cincinnati, 178; facilities, 181

Laflin, Mrs.: case story of, 155

Latham, George: case story of, 137

Legal separation to protect wife, 127-129

Legislation: irregular unions, 29, 98; pioneering methods, 50-52; state aid to mothers, 63; common law unions, legality of, 98, 101; Italian, 100; divorce for permanent desertion, 110; for justifiable deserters, 111-112; court action for persistent deserters, 114-117; extradition, 117-119, 129; probation, 120-124; legal facilities to promote efficiency, 164-184; serving a warrant, 168; extradition treaties, 169-170; deportation, 171; court procedure, 172-177; juvenile delinquency, 177, 178, 180; domestic relations, and special courts, 177, 178, 179, 180-182; marriage laws, 186, 195

Loane, M., 154

Long, Martin: case story of, 141

Making the Deserter Pay the Piper. W. H. Baldwin, 177

Mancini, Onofrio: case story of, 172

Marital vagaries: possible reasons for, 35

Marriage: spiritual values of, 11, 12, 29; homelier elements in, 13-15; wrong bases of, 28; common law unions, 29; disparagement of ideals condemned, 45-46, 198; verification, and state legislation, 98-100; registration in Italy, 100; American marriage laws, 186

McCann, Herbert: case story of, 84-85, 86

Medical-social work: preventing desertion, 9; summary of case analyses, 22; psychiatry and mental deficiency, 24; physical debility, 34; "pregnancy desertion," 34-35; sex incompatibility, 37-39; bureaus of advice recommended, 193-196. See also *Psychology*

Mellor, Joseph: case story of, 111

Mentality: irresponsible agents, 17-20; psychology of insanity, 20, 24; educational handicaps, 29

Mexico: and extradition, 119, 170

Morgan, Charles: case story of, 147-148

Motion, J. R., 171

Myers, Hiram, 191, 192

Narcotics: percentage of influence, 22, 42

Nationality: statistical facts about difference in, 26-27, 44-45; racial attitude, and percentages of deserters, 44-45; case problem, 49; Jewish desertion bureau, 65, 69, 71, 101-102

National Conference of Jewish Charities, seeks extradition treaty, 169

National Conference of Social Work, extradition treaty urged, 169

National Desertion Bureau, Jewish legal aid, 65; story of tracing a deserter, 69-70; collusive desertion cases, 71; clearing bureau established, 101-102

Neighborhood influence, see *Standards*

Newspapers, see *Publicity*

INDEX

New York Association for Improving the Condition of the Poor: practice of Desertion Bureau, 136

New York Charity Organization Society: study of racial groups, and percentages, 44-45

New York State Conference of Charities and Correction, Proceedings, on non-supporters, 150

Non-supporters: as potential deserters, 149-163; legal treatment of, 149-150; analogous to deserters, 150-153, 188; characteristics, 151, 189, 190; wife's influence a factor, 152-154; illustrations, 155, 158, 160; reclamation, illustrated, 161-163; approach to desertion, 188-191

Non-support Law: in Massachusetts, 149-150

Normal Family, The. Margaret F. Byington, 12

North of Boston. Robert Frost, 14

One Thousand Homeless Men. Alice W. Solenberger, 157

Overindulgence: teaching self-control, 25-26; wage-earning wives, 154

Pelligrini, Orfeo: case story of, 99

Permanence of family life, 9, 11-15

Permanent desertions, see *Divorce*

Philadelphia Court of Domestic Relations, report on reconciliations, 135-136

Philadelphia Society for Organizing Charity: report of, 7

Photographs of deserters: society presents to wife, 10; tracing out-of-town clues, 78, 84, 85

Physical condition: ill health, 34; "difficulty" of pregnant women, 35; maladjustments, 38; recreation essential, 47; recommendations, 196-199

"Pregnancy desertion": how explained, 34-35

Preventive treatment: past opinions, 187; non-support leading to desertion, 188-192; for first desertions, 192-193; bureaus for advice and consultation, 193-199; suggestions for, 196-199

Probation: testimony of social workers, 119-120; and imprisonment, 121-124; legal separation proceedings during 128; officers effect reconciliation, 132; illustrations, 133-134, 137, 141; "stay-away" probation, 138; economy plan for officers, 178; number and efficiency of officers, 182-184; consultation bureau, 193

Provisional quality of desertions 9

Psychoanalysis: mental deficients, and heredity, 24; incompatibility and sex perversion, 37-39. See also *Sex factors*

Psychology: rationalization process, 20; mental defectives, 24; sex incompatibility, 37-39; studies on, 39; knowledge of, essential, 103

Publicity: photographs a medium of, 10, 78, 84, 85; agencies and newspapers, 84-90; divorce by "publication," 101; illustration, 196

Queen's Poor, The. M. Loane, 154

Questionnaires: liberal relief policy, 62; searching for deserters, 78; treatment of desertion, 106

INDEX

Ratio of desertions: economic factors, 21, 31, 32-33

Reconciliation: factors that prompt, 13-14; and the "other woman," 40-41; following court marriage, 95-96; after prison term, 108-109; considerations involved, 125-132; unwillingness of wife, illustrated, 131; criminal tendencies prevent, 134; affection a safe basis of, 135; practice of N. Y. Association for Improving Condition of the Poor, 136-137; volunteer visitors helpful, 139-140; case worker's success in effecting, illustrated, 142-148; bureaus to promote, 193-199

Recreation: why essential, 47

Red Cross Home Service, 81, 159, 160

Relatives: interference of, 43-44, 49

Religion: differences in, a study of, 26, 27

Repeated desertions: frequency of, 8; "intermittent husbands," 43, 153; suggestions for tracing the man, 79; relative nature of, 92

Responsibility: self-therapy illustrated, 8; deserters disclaim, 19-20; essentials of early training, 25-26; education promotes, 29, 198; and charitable relief, 48, 100; wage-earning wives, and non-supporters, 154

Richmond, Mary E.: on volunteers in case work, 78, 106, 140

Ridicule: of matrimony, by press and films, 45-46

Russell Sage Foundation, study, American marriage laws, 186

Selective Service Act, 165

Sex factors: determine forgiveness, 13-14; statistical summary, 21-22; "pregnancy desertion," 34-35; incompatibility, 37-40; immorality, 39, 96; knowledge of sex psychology essential, 103

Sex in Relation to Society. Havelock Ellis, 39

Sexual Question, The. A. Forel, 39

Seybert Institution, Philadelphia, on relation of income to court order, 173

Slacker marriages, 97

Social workers: opinions of, 7-8 appreciative faculties of, 11; knowledge of sex relations imperative, 37-38; diagnoses referred to specialists, 38; undervalue recreation, 47; questionnaires on treatment, 62, 78, 106; detective methods, 68-90; agency co-operation, 78-90; sex problems, 103; necessary information for, summarized, 104-105; protection of legal separation, 127; successful case records, 142-148

Solenberger, Alice W., 157

Spiritual values: of family life, 11-12, 29

Standards: and temperamental differences, 36; community concepts, 45-46; neighborhood influence, 47, 102

State aid to mothers, 63; vital statistics, 93

Temporary desertions: report of Philadelphia Society, 7-8; domestic crises and vagaries, 34-35. See also *Reconciliation*

Theories to explain desertion, 20. See also *Causal factors*

Treatment of desertion: policy, past and present, 50-64; court

INDEX

intervention, 50–54; interviewing the man, 55–60, 105; relief to families, 61; opinions of case workers, 62; case story, 62; state aid, 63; closing the case, time for, 63; changes in worker's attitudes, 64; whereabouts known, willing to return, 125–148; Philadelphia Court of Domestic Relations, study by, 135–136; N. Y. Association for Improving Condition of the Poor, practice of, 136; family restoration illustrated, 137; volunteers recommended, 139–140; wife relents, illustration of reconciliation, 141; study of successful worker's records, 142–148

nited Hebrew Charities, 71

Vagaries: marital, 34–35

Venereal disease: relation to desertion, 41

Verification: of marriage, 98–99; in Italy, 100; Latin-American custom, 100

Volunteers: service valuable for effecting reconciliation, 139–140

Wanderlust: instability of temperament, 19; relation to desertion, 32

Warrant for arrest: protection afforded wife, 127; system inadequate, 168

West, Alfred: case story of, 30

Wife and Family Desertion: Emigration as a Contributory Cause. J. R. Motion, 171

Wife who deserts, not considered, 15

Williams, Mrs. Clara: case story of, 57–60, 111